Cooking
My Way
through Life
with Kids
and Books

Cooking My Way through Life with Kids and Books

Judy Alter

State🦌House Press

Buffalo Gap, Texas

Library of Congress Cataloging-in-Publication Data

Alter, Judy.
  Cooking my way through life with kids and books / Judy Alter.
    p. cm.
  Includes index.
  ISBN 978-1-933337-33-3
  1. Cookery, American. 2. Alter, Judy. I. Title.
TX715.A5035 2008
641.5973--dc22

                                                        2008049441

State House Press
P.O. Box 818
Buffalo Gap, TX 79508
(325) 572-3974
www.mcwhiney.org/press

Distributed by Texas A&M University Press Consortium
(800) 826-8911
www.tamu.edu/upress

Printed in the United States of America

ISBN 978-1-933337-33-3

Book designed by Rosenbohm Graphic Design

Cover: Jacob Shaddix Burton, age two, 2008
Photo taken by Lil' Angels Photography
Deryck and Michelle Jernigan
972-899-8805

Dedication

For my mom, who started me on the road to food and fun; for Colin, Megan, Jamie, and Jordan, who saw me through the casserole years and still seem to think I'm a pretty good cook; and for all my grandchildren—may they, too, have lives filled with love and good food.

Contents

Author's Apology of Sorts

Most cookbook recipes are kitchen-tested over and over again by experts. I confess that these recipes have been tested by me—and a few friends and relatives with whom I've shared them over the years. But they don't come with any sort of "seal of approval" (other than my friends and family) and mostly they presume that you know a bit about cooking.

Recently I tried to tell my youngest daughter Jordan about making a basic white sauce over the phone, and she said, "I can't do that. Tell me something else to do with these meatballs." Another time I told a friend to make a basic powdered sugar icing, and he said, "Wait! You have to understand. I don't know what you're talking about." In a lot of these recipes, while I've tried to be clear, I do assume you know what I'm talking about. To me, improvisation is the great part about cooking, and especially in recent years, I've loved experimenting, twisting this recipe and adapting that one.

Questions? Email me at judy@judyalter.com, and I'll do my best to help.

Preface

When good friend Sheila Taylor Wells said, half jokingly, "We should write a cookbook together," I took her seriously. I think she was probably dismayed at the time, for I immediately sat down and pounded out 5,000 words about my childhood. Then I began persistently to ask Sheila, "Have you put pen to paper yet?"

Finally we had a "working dinner," and the truth came out. Sheila is a recent convert to cooking, whereas food always has been a big part of my life. As she bemoaned that she didn't have as much to say as I do (usually the opposite is true), I said, "Well, surely you've got your mom's recipes."

"Mom didn't cook."

Stumped silence. Then: "Well, how did you feed your children?"

"I took them out."

I was beginning to see her point.

Sheila decided that I should continue to write the memoir/cookbook, and her contribution would be to write commentary, to react to what I'd written. Since she's one of the best and funniest writers I know, I thought that was a great idea. Sheila's been a columnist for papers in several cities, including our hometown, Fort Worth. If she wrote commentary, I'd go soaring into heights of culinary and family bliss, and Sheila would bring me right back down to earth. When someone asked what Sheila was going to write, I said, "Rebuttal."

But after two or three weeks, she said it wasn't working. She'd tried, and nothing came out right. It was my book and should be.

The truth is that two of my dreams have long been to own a restaurant and to write a cookbook. About the former: I know therein lies disaster, so for a long time I scratched that itch by helping out once a week at The Star Café, located in Fort Worth's Stockyards National Historic District and owned by good friends Don and Betty Boles. Specialties of the house are steak, chicken-fried steak, and really good hamburgers. I ran the cash register, visited with guests, rolled endless quantities of silverware, and got to see both the fun of restaurant life and its perils. I'm not going down that road, but I liked my Saturday nights.

But the cookbook! That dream probably comes from the fact that I've been a book person all my life. I wrote my first short stories when I was ten or twelve—my mother saved them, and I have them still. In high school, I wrote a short story and sent it to *Seventeen,* the bible for girls my age at that time. It came back with alarming speed. But I've gone on to have a most satisfying career as an author and publisher (even though, as I hasten to tell schoolchildren, I'm neither rich nor famous), and almost any topic presents itself to me as a potential book—or not. I've written some sixty books, which is not really as impressive as it sounds—many were short children's books written on assignment for companies that sell to school libraries. But I have had novels, both adult and young adult, published in New York and Texas, and I've won some nice awards, including Wranglers from the National Cowboy Hall of Fame, Spurs from Western Writers of America, and—praise be!—an Owen Wister Award for Lifetime Achievement from Western Writers in 2005. As a good friend once suggested, I've had more success than most writers can expect.

Food has always been important to me. Like my faith, it sustains me. It is part of my self-assumed role as a nurturer—I love to feed people—and it's a big factor in my social life. I'd rather go out to dinner with friends or have them into my house than go to the theater or a movie. At the table, there's sociability and interchange and friendship; at the theater or the symphony, each person is pretty well isolated until afterward, when talk may flow in comparing reactions.

For me, food is also about continuity—and change. I bring to the table today the recipes of my mother, still often used and some, I'm sure, from her mother. I bring a few from my ex-husband's Jewish tradition. So my cooking preserves the past and carries it on for my children and grand-children.

But cooking is also about change. Now seventy (can that be true?), I've seen a lot of changes in what we Americans eat. I've seen fast food mushroom beyond belief and the family dinner hour almost disappear—both trends I bemoan. I've seen foods come and go—remember when the "in thing" was to order fondue at a fancy restaurant? But not many eat fondue today, although I hear it's making a comeback.

In the '80s there was all that fuss about crepes—whole restaurants devoted to them—and quiche, and the book *Real Men Don't Eat Quiche*. Pasta changed from spaghetti and meatballs to all kind of exciting things, beginning with fettuccine Alfredo and moving on to goat cheese pizza. Italian food in the United States today is much more sophisticated than lasagna, and that's a good thing, though I still love lasagna.

Pretty much gone are the Chinese restaurants of my youth, with chrome and Formica furniture and little white take-out boxes (not that I ate at them very often—Chinese was not on my dad's list of acceptable foods). Today, we eat pan-Asian food—Thai, Vietnamese, everything from glass noodles to sushi and sashimi (which I love)—but who would have eaten raw fish in the '60s?

Hamburgers have morphed from a meat patty on a bun with lettuce, tomato, onion, and mustard into imaginative concoctions of which guacamole and bacon are the least exotic additions. We've added game to our menus, and now the trendiest restaurants serve elk tacos, venison medallions, wild boar chops, and buffalo hamburgers.

I'm a believer in experimenting with the new foods, and I'm as ready as anyone to try a seared scallop on a bed of pureed cauliflower (even though I don't much like cauliflower) and topped with foie gras (it was probably the best tapa I've ever had). But I also think it's important to carry on the recipes of the past—King Ranch chicken and meatloaf and tuna casserole, albeit with a twist. In many ways, the path of my life with food—and kids and books—traces the ways that our food has changed in this country and yet, I hope, emphasizes the importance of keeping tradition.

I began thinking about the different foods that had been in my life at different times: a sheltered child in a middle-class, slightly British household; a young adult who married into a new culture and moved to another new one; a single parent of four; and now an older adult, living alone and entertaining often.

A disclaimer here: I am not a gourmet cook. My friends all call me that, and one who has traveled the world often says she's never had better meals than she has at my house. But I know better. I use prepared ingredients—I'm not above admitting that I use Campbell's soup in some recipes, and have for years. When a recipe says "the finest French chocolate," I use Baker's if I have it on hand. I figure my friends and I can't really tell the difference, and, frankly, I don't have time to make my own pasta, and I often don't have the money for French chocolate. So I fudge in ways that a true gourmet never would. I also use shortcuts, and I cook ahead of time rather than killing myself trying to coordinate a meal by preparing everything at the last minute for freshness. True gourmets would discount my cooking—but my friends and guests love it. So maybe my story is how a busy woman with a limited budget can still come off as a gourmet cook.

My children—Colin, Megan, Jamie, and Jordan—are mentioned often in these pages, and I think food is a bond we share. When my daughters married, each received a loose-leaf notebook with Mom's recipes. Of course, the recipes varied wildly because Megan hates a beef casserole I make and Jordan loves it; Megan won't touch cream cheese, which Jordan would eat three times a day if it weren't so fattening; Megan is more adventuresome about new foods and tastes, and for Megan, the hotter the better, while Jordan shies away from jalapenos and other chilies. And so it goes. At our frequent family get-togethers—there are now nine adults and seven grandchildren, ranging from nine to one—what to fix for supper is the center of the celebration. (We do eat a lot of fajitas!) When I mentioned this cookbook/memoir, each of my children had suggestions. "Remember when you used to fix. . ."

(Note: Colin is married to Lisa; their children are Morgan and Kegan. Megan is married to Brandon, and they have two boys: Sawyer and Ford.

Jamie is married to Melanie, and their daughters are Maddie and Edie, also known as Beastie. And Jordan is married to Christian; they're the parents of Jacob, the grandchild who lives closest to me.)

Other people mentioned frequently in these pages—besides my mother, my brother John, and my ex-husband, Joel—are Uncle Bob and Bobbie. Uncle Bob told people he was my brother, though he wasn't. I took to calling him my shirt-tail brother, a term that I thought I'd heard but one that puzzled everyone else. He came into our lives when I took a macramé class from him (does that date me!), and he gradually began to drop by the house. Sometimes he'd bring his current lover—they changed constantly—and they, too, became family, however briefly.

When Joel moved on, Uncle Bob became a fixture in the children's lives. They were his children, the children that his gay lifestyle would never let him have. He adored them, and if they can drive a car or ride a horse today, it's because of Uncle Bob. Uncle Bob died of AIDS in 1994. None of us have forgiven him yet, but we also grieve for him and treasure his memory. All of us have pieces of his art—paper art, paintings, weavings—in our homes.

In the late '80s or early '90s, I joined a group of women whose lives revolved around books, as mine did. They were librarians, booksellers, and authors who met for breakfast once a month. I was a founding member of the group. Some of the women began to tell me over and over that I really should meet Bobbie Simms because I had so much in common with her and would really like her. I actually began to bristle a little: who was this Bobbie Simms anyway?

Turns out she owned an antiquarian bookstore close to my home and was retired after years of teaching English at a local university. And when we met, we hit it off. Bobbie was thirteen years older than me, part mother, part soul mate. She often wrote me notes, once about how remarkable it is to get a soul mate late in life. "Here I am experiencing the joy of the freedom to speak of *whatever* with you." For a book group that I was leading at TCU, she read a book she hated and wrote, "Only love for you kept me at it."

Bobbie, once a heavy smoker, developed chronic obstructive pulmonary disease. Eventually she was on oxygen eighteen hours a day. She refused to leave the house with a portable oxygen tank, but my, oh my! did she make use of her six hours of daily freedom. We lunched, we shopped, we explored, and we had a wonderful time. When she unexpectedly died in her sleep, she was in the midst of planning to attend Colin's wedding on Grand Cayman Island. When I said to her, "I know you can't attend," she snapped, "I don't know. I just may be there." Colin was making arrangements to get oxygen for her. My children came from all over Texas for her funeral.

Bobbie is buried, now next to her husband, in the same cemetery as my mother. I have visions of the two of them talking about me, and sometimes when I drive by, I say: "Hey, ladies!"

So here it is—the story of my life, which has been a rich one, and the story of what I cook when I'm up, when I'm down, and when—oh, blessed moment—my kids and grandkids come to visit!

Chapter I

A Meat-and-Potatoes Household

Chicago, the city of my birth, boasted one of the nation's biggest and busiest stockyards when I was growing up. I can remember summer evenings in our Hyde Park neighborhood when the wind shifted just so and the smell of the stockyards drifted over us. And I can remember being taken by our rather well-to-do but childless neighbors, whom I called Uncle Jack and Auntie E., to the stockyards for dinner at a "club" where each diner could brand his own steak. I wasn't much of a steak eater and would ask if they had fish. Auntie E., a devout Catholic, would say, "It's not Friday. You don't have to eat fish."

But Chicago, "the hog butcher of the world," according to poet Carl Sandburg, was an appropriate place for my Canadian-born father to land because it had a lot of beef as well as pork. He was very British in his attitudes about food—and many other things. He even had an accent, pronouncing *khaki* "kharki" and putting a droll sound on *doll*. As patriarch of the household, he set the course for the way we ate—and we ate meat and potatoes. No fish. (Mom used to be embarrassed when she dragged him to seafood restaurants in Boston and he ordered beef.) No fried chicken—in fact, nothing that you picked up with your hands except a sandwich for lunch—never dinner. He'd have hated artichokes, which I didn't even know about until I was grown.

Mom, me, Granny Peterman, the German cook in the family

Dad was a physician, college president, and hospital administrator. He walked a mile plus some to work each morning, home at lunch for a twenty-minute nap, back again, and home in the evening. Each night after that walk, when he got home, he went upstairs and put on a fresh white shirt for dinner.

Mom was of German descent; her maiden name was Peterman. Her parents were first-generation Americans, and she'd had to eat so much sauerkraut when she was a child that it never appeared in our house. Little German food did, although late in her life she loved sausage. I can't be sure, but I think she retained a few cooking habits from her childhood. Of course, she never wrote these recipes down, but I remember a few dishes distinctly. When she made meatloaf, she used a mixture of hamburger and ground pork sausage with, I suppose, a little bread and salt and pepper—none of the ketchup and other things that go into today's meatloaf made with canned "fixin's." She also made a sausage and apple skillet.

SAUSAGE AND APPLE SKILLET

1 lb. ground pork sausage

2-3 tart apples, cored and cut into slices but not peeled

Fry pork sausage until crumbled and done; drain off some of the grease and add two or three sliced apples—maybe McIntosh? I would presume a tart variety—and cook until apples are mushy. (Also, in those days we didn't have choices between hot or mild or maple-flavored sausage. There was only what today would be labeled "regular" or "original.")

And maybe wilted lettuce came from Granny Peterman's kitchen.

WILTED LETTUCE
2-3 slices bacon cooked crisp and crumbled – save 2 Tbsp. grease
Vinegar to taste (start with 1 tsp. and taste)
Fresh leaf lettuce
Mom would fry bacon, drain some of the grease off and add vinegar to the remaining, and crumble the bacon into it and reheat until just warm. Then she poured it over leaf lettuce that was always fresh from Dad's garden.

Mom also used to fix beets and greens, which you almost never see these days. I don't think people eat fresh beets much—or any other kind. She'd cook the beets, slice them, and return them to the pan with the washed and stemmed greens until the greens were soft. She always poured vinegar over beets and greens, and one of my sons always ate them that way. I prefer them with butter and lemon. But a warning: it's hard to find enough greens on fresh beets.

BEETS AND GREENS
1 bunch fresh beets with full, healthy greens still attached
Butter
Lemon and butter or vinegar to taste
Remove greens from beets; wash and set aside. Boil beets until they can easily be pierced with a fork. Run under cold water until cool enough to handle and peel (the peel slips right off once cooked). Cut off the ends, slice, and return to drained saucepan. Trim stems off greens and add to pan with just a bit of moisture. Cook until beets are heated and greens are wilted and cooked. Serve with butter and lemon or vinegar.

I never ate southern dishes as a "northern" kid, but it occurs to me all these years later that Mom's fried mush was typically southern. I think fried mush was one more thing from my Granny Peterman's kitchen.

FRIED MUSH

Cornmeal

Oil

Butter

Syrup

Make cornmeal mush in a loaf pan, following directions on the cornmeal, and chill. (Today, we'd call it hard polenta.) Slice and fry in skillet with small amount of oil or maybe she used margarine (I'd use butter today). Serve warm with butter and syrup. It's delicious! A great breakfast.

Mom was very much a pre-Betty Freidan '50s housewife. She might have wanted to work—she held a degree from the University of Chicago and had once been secretary to Robert Hutchins, chancellor of the University of Chicago and originator of the Great Books program—but Dad would have been embarrassed if his wife went to work. So she did volunteer work and kept our household running to his satisfaction. And every evening just before Dad got home, she changed into a fresh dress, sprayed on some perfume, and combed her hair. She set a formal table in the dining room, and we ate on a linen tablecloth and had that relic of the past, napkin rings. And every night, Dad asked grace before dinner.

A few things that Mom cooked reflect Dad's British influence. She served both sliced, sautéed mushrooms and steamed asparagus on buttered toast— very British. One of my sons loves asparagus on toast—and so do I.

Mom loved fish, but the only fish I remember her cooking was halibut, which she smothered in milk and baked. I don't think I much liked it. As a child, I ate a lot of canned tuna, straight from the can with only a little lemon.

We were required to eat liver for our health. I know I hated it, and I'm pretty sure my brother, John, did too. We tried every way we knew to avoid it. Ironically, now that we've found out that (contrary to the belief of our childhood) it's not good for you because the liver essentially is a filter to remove toxins from the system, I can cook it so that I like it.

SAUTÉED LIVER

1 lb. calf's liver

Lemon juice

2 Tbsp. butter, or more as needed

1 medium onion, diced

Sprinkle liver with lemon juice. Sauté onion in butter in a skillet. Add liver (and more butter if you need it) and barely cook—you want it almost rare in the middle, but not quite. Overcooked liver becomes leather—not a good thing. Use more lemon juice to deglaze the pan, and then pour it over the liver. (The lemon juice cuts that gamy taste.) Recipe serves three generously or four tentative liver eaters.

If I resented the liver meals, I liked two other unusual meats that were on the menu. Mom would boil a corned beef tongue for dinner, sometimes with potatoes and cabbage, and to this day I like a good tongue sandwich. But I have lunch companions who almost have to look away when I order it at the local deli. Once at John's house, years ago, his then-wife served tongue, and as he carved it, John rolled his tongue around outside his mouth. Not a child would eat it.

Mom and me in the kitchen in our big house, before we remodeled it.

Mom also served kidneys—and today we know they're no better for you than liver. I never see them in the stores. Mom cooked lamb kidneys—never beef, which are too tough and big. She floured them as you might chicken. She'd fry some bacon and then cook the kidneys in the bacon grease. This is great with ketchup. Once, years later, I made a steak-and-kidney pie, but we had dinner guests who wouldn't eat it.

Mom was great about encouraging me to cook, and at a fairly young age I was making peanut butter cookies or chocolate chip cookies. (I liked the dough as well as the baked cookies.) I remember one time when a girl-friend and I were cooking something—who knows what?—and a childless friend of Mom's came by. The kitchen was a mess; I hadn't learned yet the art of cleaning up as I go, which is now almost a religious practice with me. The friend asked Mom quietly, "How can you let them make such a mess?" And Mom said, "If I don't, they'll never learn to cook."

One time I made a chocolate cake that I proudly served to my parents, assuring them that I had carefully followed the recipe. It tasted awful, sort of like Alka Seltzer. "Judy, how much baking soda did you put in?" Mom asked.

"Nine teaspoons," I replied.

"Nine teaspoons!" But then she looked at the recipe, and there was an error in it. I had indeed followed it carefully—I just wasn't yet smart enough about cooking to know the disastrous effect that nine teaspoons of baking soda would have. Needless to say, we threw the cake out.

As part of her volunteer work, Mom edited a cookbook, called *Tasty Treasures,* for the hospital auxiliary. I still have it and use it today. But Mom thought it needed more recipes, and she didn't think it looked good to have too many recipes by Alice MacBain, so she adapted the pen name of Penelope Jones. Here are a couple of Penelope Jones' recipes—though dated, they are still good.

APPLE RELISH

    1 lb. large red apples

    2 dill pickles

    1 medium onion

    ½ cup sugar

    ¼ cup vinegar

    Core apples, but do not peel. Grind together with pickles and onions. Add sugar and vinegar. Serve chilled with meats.

FRUIT SALAD DRESSING

2 Tbsp. melted butter

2 Tbsp. flour

3 eggs, separated

½ c. sugar

Dash of salt

¼ c. pineapple juice

1 c. whipped cream

Melt butter in double boiler and add flour. Add egg yolks, sugar, and salt. Cook until thick. Stir in 2 egg whites beaten medium and cook 5 minutes. Remove from heat and add lukewarm pineapple juice and whipped cream.

When Mom contributed a guacamole recipe under her own name, she felt compelled to explain guacamole as "avocado paste." (After all, we were northerners.) Wouldn't Mom be surprised by our current familiarity with guacamole and tortilla chips?

GUACAMOLE

2 ripe avocados

½ tsp. salt

2 tsp. lime juice

Dash of cayenne

1 Tbsp. finely minced onion

Dash of Worcestershire sauce

Mash avocados. Add lime juice and blend into smooth paste. Add seasoning and mix lightly. Chill and serve on lettuce leaves. (Her note says this may also be used as a "dunking" sauce—not quite how we think of guacamole today.)

Mom also added some "Gourmet Grace" suggestion sidebars, such as "A slice of apple in your cooky [sic] jar will keep soft cookies moist and mellow" or "If you like nuts all in one piece, soak them in salt water overnight before cracking." Gourmet Grace also suggested stirring a tablespoon of orange juice into each egg before scrambling and adding a pinch of basil to beaten eggs for an omelet.

A number of recipes are in handwriting that looks suspiciously like Mom's but bear the names of other women, mostly my aunts. But that cookbook was where I first burst into print with a recipe for a dip.

HOT PARTY DIP
    1-2 garlic cloves
    1 can cream of mushroom soup
    ¼ c. boiling water
    1 bouillon cube
    6 oz. cheese, preferably Velveeta, cubed
    1 egg
    Crush garlic into a double boiler; add soup and bouillon cube dissolved in ¼ c. boiling water. (The recipe originally called for a link of garlic-flavored cheese, but I don't see those in the store today and use Velveeta and extra garlic.) Cook until cheese melts. Finally drop in one egg. Beat until well blended. Serve hot.
    And there it is, my signature: Judy MacBain

I used to make a cheese dip that was much admired by some, although I don't remember the exact ingredients, and it came out differently every time I tried it. Once, when I was in high school, on request, I gave the recipe to Dad's executive assistant, for whom I was working at the time. She served it to her current boyfriend and promptly accused me of trying to sabotage her love life. Later, she softened enough to say that I was the only one who could make it work. I've seen similar recipes in cooking magazines today.

CHEESE DIP

Blue cheese

Cottage cheese

Mayonnaise or sour cream or a combination of both

Dash of Worcestershire sauce

Pinch of dry mustard

Chopped scallions

You have to experiment with proportions. I don't think I used cream cheese, but it might be a good addition. I did this in the blender (before we had food processors).

I learned little tricks from Mom, like making slits in a roast and stuffing slivers of garlic into them, or marinating the cooked potatoes for potato salad in Italian dressing before adding the onion, celery, mustard, and mayonnaise.

And I remember a few ordinary meals. For instance, Mom, with a frugality born of the Depression, served us Spam. She'd score the top, cover it with brown sugar, stud it with cloves just like a ham, and bake it, or sometimes she'd slice it and fry. I still like it, though I find the fat content pretty scary.

The other day I mentioned that I had fixed myself some corned beef hash, and Colin asked if I'd put the can in the refrigerator first. Then he explained to son-in-law Christian that I used to chill the hash, open both ends of the can, and push the hash out as a cylinder. Then you can slice it and fry patties to serve with ketchup—still a favorite of mine. I'd forgotten that I did that when he was young, but it was a trick I learned from Mom.

Sunday nights in the winter we ate in front of the fireplace in the living room. Mom had a tea cart that had been given to them as a wedding present—it's now an occasional table in my living room—and she'd roll it into the living room. My parents would each sit in their own chairs, while John and I perched on footstools. We ate things like the cheese sandwich soufflé or spinach soufflé.

Spinach soufflé deserves its own mention. I don't have her recipe and wish I did. Recently at a B&B in Oregon I was served spinach strata for breakfast, and I wrote to ask if the owners would share the recipe, but I got no reply. I'm sure Mom used canned spinach, cheddar cheese, and eggs. I loved it. John hated it. Now in his seventies, he still remembers one night when it was served at the dining room table. He took one bite and was instantly sick. Dad decided that he should sit there until he ate it. So the rest of us finished dinner and left the table—and there sat John. (I don't know the outcome, whether or not he ever ate it.) Mom said to me in her later years, "Wasn't that an awful thing to do to a child?"

SPINACH SOUFFLÉ THAT SOUNDS CLOSE TO MOM'S

1 16-oz. bag frozen spinach, thawed and squeezed dry

¼ c. butter

¼ c. flour

½ tsp. salt

⅛ tsp. ground black pepper

1 c. milk

2 Tbsp. finely chopped onion

½ tsp. salt

⅛ tsp. ground nutmeg

3 large eggs, separated

¼ tsp cream of tartar

Heat oven to 350° and butter a quart casserole dish. Heat butter in saucepan, add flour, and stir until smooth. Add salt and pepper. Gradually add milk, stirring constantly. When thick, remove from heat and stir in onion, remaining salt and nutmeg.

In separate bowl, beat egg whites and cream of tartar until stiff peaks form. In separate bowl, beat yolks until lemony. Stir yolks into sauce; stir in spinach. Put ¼ of egg whites into spinach fixture. Fold in gently and then add remaining whites.

Pour into dish, set in large pan of water (about 1 inch depth) and bake 50-60 minutes. Top will brown lightly. Serve immediately.

On the other hand, my brother recently asked me how Mom used to make Welsh rarebit, another Sunday night favorite. Welsh rarebit is no relation to rabbit; the name comes from the Welsh *caws pobi*, which literally means rare (barely cooked) and *bit* (as in a small serving.)

WELSH RAREBIT

1½ cups sharp cheddar cheese, grated

2 Tbsp. beer (Mom probably split the rest of the beer with Dad; with strong and recent memories of the Depression, she could never have thrown it out. You can substitute milk, but it's not as good.)

1 tsp. dried mustard

Pepper to taste

Melt cheese and beer in saucepan, add pepper and mustard. Most recipes call for serving it over buttered toast and running it under the broiler to brown it, but Mom served it on saltine crackers, and I don't recall that she broiled it. I have also seen a version—called Scotch woodcock, I think—that added tomatoes. It is a light supper, so much so that when I served it once to my family, Colin asked incredulously, "This is dinner?"

Cheese sandwich soufflé was another Sunday night favorite. Today we might call it strata.

CHEESE SANDWICH SOUFFLÉ

8 slices of bread

¼ lb. sharp cheddar, sliced, or more

4 eggs, beaten lightly

2 cups milk

½ tsp. salt

Dash each of pepper, paprika, and cayenne

Trim crust from bread. Place 4 slices in bottom of buttered casserole. Slice cheese over bread. Cover with additional 4 slices of bread. Add eggs to milk; add, salt, pepper, paprika, and cayenne. Pour milk mixture over casserole. Chill in refrigerator all day or overnight. Bake in moderate oven 350° for 35 minutes or until puffed up and brown. Thorough chilling makes for puffing. Serves four.

Mom and Dad entertained a lot, whether for Dad's professional needs or groups of close friends. I learned a lot from those dinner parties. By the time I was twelve, I was Mom's first assistant. I'd serve hors d'oeuvres, and while the guests were dining, I cleaned the kitchen. At the end of the evening, when the last guest had been bid farewell, I had the kitchen cleaned up. Of course, there was the night that Dad thought his guests were overstaying their welcome and got out the vacuum cleaner, to Mom's eternal mortification.

I don't remember a lot of what she cooked on those occasions, but two recipes stick in my mind: stuffed mushrooms as an appetizer and leg of lamb cooked with port wine.

STUFFED MUSHROOMS
Large mushroom caps
Sharp cheddar cheese, about a tsp. per mushroom cap
Dash of Worcestershire
Chopped scallions
Pinch of dry mustard (too much gives it an odd flavor)
Enough mayonnaise to bind
Clean mushroom caps (I finally learned to use a damp paper towel and not soak them in saltwater the way Mom did). Shred sharp cheddar cheese. Add a bit of Worcestershire, dry mustard, and chopped scallion. Add mayonnaise. Stuff mushroom caps. Bake in a moderate oven until mushrooms are cooked and soft and cheese has melted.. If the cheese has not browned, you may run it under the broiler. But the baking is important; if you just broil, you'll melt the cheese but have crisp, raw mushrooms.

PORT WINE LEG OF LAMB

   1 onion, sliced thin

   2 tsp. each salt, pepper, and allspice

   Leg of lamb, bone in

   2 bay leaves

   1 c. water

   1 c. dark berry or grape jam

   ½ c. vinegar

   Port wine

Dip each onion slice in spice mixture. Cut slits in the lamb and insert pieces of onion. Roast the leg of lamb with two bay leaves and water and sprinkle remaining salt, pepper, and allspice over the lamb. Bake one hour covered at 350°. Add vinegar to juices in pan and spread jam over roast. Finish roasting (3 hours at 325°) uncovered, basting frequently.

Make a gravy using flour and port wine—no water. Mom used to make gravy—turkey, for instance—by putting cold water in a small Mason jar, dumping in an equal amount of flour, and shaking vigorously. She'd stir this into the hot drippings, and it came out almost lump-free. Today we can do it in a food processor, but I suspect that the same technique would work with the port, particularly if you chilled it first.

We had traditional foods for holidays. We always had cold turkey and potato salad, by personal request, on my birthday. And for Thanksgiving we had turkey with "northern" stuffing—no cornbread stuffing for us, though Mom had an old iron cornbread pan that made bread sticks that looked like ears of corn, and we loved those. We had mashed potatoes, sweet potatoes seasoned with bourbon and topped with miniature marshmallows, cranberry relish, probably green beans, always a tossed salad (one of Mom's specialties), and pumpkin pie for dessert. Christmas was pretty much the same menu.

SWEET POTATOES

Sweet potatoes – as many as you need, count on one large potato feeding two people, since there will be so much else on the plates.

Butter, to taste

Bourbon, to taste

Salt and pepper, to taste

Miniature marshmallows

Cook sweet potatoes and mash with plenty of butter; add bourbon to taste, along with a bit of salt and pepper. Cover with marshmallows and bake until warm through and marshmallows are brown and melted. (A friend once said to me, "Don't you ruin my sweet potatoes with bourbon," but these were really good.)

Mom made a fresh cranberry relish that I love to this day and often make on holidays. There's almost no way to make a small amount, and you always have too much left over. Dad used an old hand grinder for this, and I can still see him grinding away. The making of the relish took an entire evening when I was a child. Today, with food processors, it's much easier.

CRANBERRY RELISH

1 1 lb. pkg. cranberries, washed and sorted

3-4 tart red apples, cored and sliced, unpeeled

1 orange, sliced but unpeeled

½ c. sugar

1 small can shredded pineapple, optional (Mom did *not* add that, but I have)

Grind cranberries, apples, and orange (or chop with off-and-on turns in food processor, but don't get too small and don't let it turn to mush—this should be coarsely textured). Add sugar to taste. Start with ½ cup and see what pleases you. Some recipes call for as much as two cups, but I don't like it that sweet.) Add pineapple last.

At Christmas we had "Krispie Orange Cookies." Mom had a store of cookie cutters in Christmas shapes: Santa Claus, a Christmas tree, a bell, a wreath. They were the good, old-fashioned kind—metal that cut cleanly through the dough as opposed to the plastic ones for sale today. I still have Mom's cutters. She'd decorate her cookies with icing and colored sugars and other things—you're only as limited as your imagination.

These are Colin's absolute favorite. He literally demands them every Christmas. Now Lisa, bless her, has taken over the somewhat labor-intensive task of making them. Colin likes these soft—not baked as long—but they were originally meant to be crisp.

KRISPIE ORANGE COOKIES

1 c. shortening

2 c. sugar

2 eggs, beaten

1 orange, rind grated, then juice the orange

1 tsp. baking powder

1 tsp. salt

3½ c. flour

Cream the shortening and sugar. Add eggs and beat. Add orange juice and grated rind. Add flour, into which you've mixed baking powder and salt. Chill at least one hour and roll out. (We always cut them into Christmas shapes and decorated them with basic powdered sugar icing and then added sprinkles or whatever.)

Bake at 375° for 10-12 minutes, watching carefully. If they begin to brown around the edgese, they're done. And use an insulated cookie sheet or if you have old-fashioned ones like I do, put another cookie sheet upside down under it so they don't burn on the bottom.

A good friend in New Mexico once asked for my coffee cake recipe, but he called to say he was baffled by basic powdered sugar icing. He needed more specific instruction. Since I've always done it by guess and by gosh, I was hard put to give him any help. But here's what I came up with:

BASIC POWDERED SUGAR ICING

    2 c. powdered sugar
    2 Tbsp. soft butter
    1 tsp. vanilla
    1 tsp. almond flavoring (optional)
    Boiling water
    Add butter and flavorings to sugar. Add boiling water carefully, a
    teaspoon at a time, beating after each addition, until icing is the right
    consistency—it should be thin enough to spread easily but not so thin
    that it runs off the cookie.

On Christmas Eve, we always went to the home of family friends. Several foods were traditional, and I don't know which ones Mom contributed and which came from other families. But two have stayed in the family. Because I'm allergic to shrimp, I don't fix the pickled shrimp any more, but it's one of the more unusual recipes I've tried. And my kids all clamor for the cheese ball.

CHEESE BALL

    ½ lb. Roquefort
    1 pkg. Old English cheese (no longer available—I use an 8-oz. pkg of
    Velveeta)
    l 8-oz. pkg. cream cheese
    ½ lb. pecans, chopped fine
    1 bunch parsley, chopped fine
    1 tsp. Worcestershire sauce
    1 small onion, chopped fine
    ½ tsp. horseradish
    Let the cheeses soften to room temperature and mix thoroughly. Add
    Worcestershire, onion, horseradish, and half of the parsley and pecans.
    Mix thoroughly and shape into a ball. (Do *not* do this in the food processor, as it will become too runny. A mixer will make it too smooth
    and creamy—wash your hands thoroughly and dig in, so the finished

cheese ball has some texture but no big chunks of cheese.) Roll the ball in the remaining parsley and pecans. Chill. Serve with crackers.

To my surprise, cheese balls develop mold if refrigerated too long. But you can freeze this one for three to four months if you're really preparing ahead for the holidays.

PICKLED SHRIMP
2½ lbs. shrimp
Shrimp boil or ½ c. celery tops, 3½ tsp. salt, and ¼ c. pickling spices
Sliced onions
7-8 bay leaves
1¼ c. salad oil
¾ c. white vinegar
1½ tsp. salt
2½ Tbsp. capers with juice
Dash of Tabasco
Cook shrimp, using shrimp boil or alternate seasonings. Drain, cool, and peel. Alternate layers of shrimp (sliced in half is best) and sliced onions in a shallow dish. Add bay leaves. Mix oil, vinegar, salt, capers, and Tabasco and pour over shrimp and onions. Cover and store in refrigerator at least 24 hours before serving. This will keep a week or more in the refrigerator.

The Christmas pièce de resistance, the one that calls back so many memories, was mom's Christmas coffee cakes. Mom would bake early in the morning on Christmas Eve, and by the time my brother and I arrived in the kitchen—why was my father never a part of this?—ten or twelve tree-shaped cakes were ready to be decorated with gumdrops, red and green cherries, silver shot, red hots, red and green sugar, and whatever else entered our fancies.

Mom was quite strict about the decorating: she beat up basic icing to just the right consistency—a little runny, but not too much so—and then dribbled it across the cakes, so it looked like a sprinkling of snow, with strict instructions to us on the order in which decorations had to go on.

Each finished cake was put on a square of cardboard—festively covered with aluminum foil—and covered with clear wrap. By late morning, we were off to deliver the cakes; I think my father became part of the tradition here, though as soon as my brother was old enough to drive, the delivering was left to the two of us.

We had a regular list of recipients, and at every house where we stopped, we were assured that Christmas morning would not be the same without one of Alice MacBain's coffee cakes. And we left the same warning, the one that every recipient already knew: don't put it in the oven to warm, because the icing will melt and the decorations will run off. Warm it on a cookie sheet on the stove or (should one be so elegant) a warming tray. And always we left with hearty Christmas wishes ringing in our ears.

Newly married and living in Texas, far from my Chicago home, I began to make Christmas coffee cakes and soon had a list of friends who counted on them. When my father died and my mother moved to Texas, she once again took over the baking. When Mother failed and we had to move her out of her home, I carefully carried home the box that held coffee cake "decorates." I told my brother that I truly felt I had inherited the family mantle.

BASIC COFFEE CAKE DOUGH

2 pkg. granular yeast

½ c. warm water

Pinch of sugar

1 12-oz. can evaporated milk, plus enough water to make 4 cups (nowadays I use "light" milk)

1 scant c. vegetable oil

1 c. sugar

Dissolve yeast in water (add just a pinch of sugar to help the yeast work) and let it rise about five minutes. Mix milk and water, oil, and sugar. Add dissolved yeast. Stir in enough flour to make a thin batter, the consistency of cake batter. Let this rise in a warm place until bubbles appear on the surface (probably 1 hour—check it at 30 minutes). Separately, mix

1 c. flour

1 tsp. salt (or less)

1 heaping tsp. baking powder

1 level tsp. baking soda

2 Tbsp. cardamom (Optional, but this makes it really good—I keep my cardamom in the freezer from year to year.)

Sift seasoned flour into first mixture. Keep adding flour until it is too stiff to stir with a spoon. Knead well. Don't let the dough get stiff with too much flour, or your coffee cakes will be heavy. This dough will keep a week or so in the refrigerator.

Also optional: coat 16 oz. candied citron with flour and mix into batter; if your family hates citron, you can substitute raisins. (Being a purist, I insist on citron over the howls of my now-grown children, who don't like raisins either—or cardamom, for that matter!)

To shape Christmas tree coffee cakes

Roll handful of dough into a log about 4-5 inches long and the size of your thumb (maybe a little bigger). Make the next roll a little shorter, and the next, and so on, until you end with a round-shaped piece of dough for the top of the tree. Add a round base for the trunk. Let rise until almost doubled in size.

To bake:

Bake at 375° for 20 minutes or until lightly browned. Cool thoroughly before decorating.

To decorate:

Make a basic powdered sugar icing (see recipe above). Flavor as you like; I use vanilla and almond flavoring, but rum might also be good. Make the icing fairly runny—you want it to drip off the spoon but not roll off the cake (tricky business, that!).

Line up all decorations before you begin. Put lighter decorations on first—silver shot, etc.—as they are more like to roll off. You can always press quartered gumdrops or halved maraschino cherries into the icing.

I suggest any or all of the following:

Green or red sugar (I like green better—it looks like a tree)

Nonpareils (those little colored things—sort of multicolored shot)

Silver or gold shot, if you can find it (tiny silver balls, not much good to eat but they look pretty)

Red or cinnamon hots (these are particularly bad about rolling off)

Halved red and green maraschino cherries

Quartered gumdrops

Anything else that strikes your fancy

Drizzle icing from a spoon over the cake in a back-and-forth motion, but don't try to cover the entire cake—you want it to look sort of like snow has blown onto the tree. Then, *quickly,* apply decorations.

You can only make Christmas coffee cakes if you intend to share them with friends! This recipe makes four large coffee cakes, but you can vary the size by the number and size of "logs" you put into the tree.

The coffeecake dough is what Mom called her "everlasting roll dough." Just leave out the cardamom and candied fruit, and you can do lots of things with it. Make cloverleaf rolls by putting three small round pieces of dough in each place in a greased muffin pan. Bake until brown (Mom said to cook them at 400°, but I think that's too hot. They brown but remain doughy in the middle.) My family likes it better when I roll the dough to a thickness of about ¼ inch, use a biscuit cutter or glass to cut out circles—I have an old tin can that Mom used and I suspect maybe Granny Peterman did, too—put a tiny bit of butter in the middle of each, and fold over. Bake on a greased cookie sheet until golden brown. Be sure to use an insulated cookie sheet or put an extra sheet under the one you're using—these burn on the bottom easily.

To make good, gooey pecan rolls for breakfast, roll the dough out to a flat rectangle. Sprinkle with cinnamon and brown sugar and dab with butter. Roll up into a tube and slice into pieces of about 2 inches. Grease the bottom of an 8x8 pan thoroughly and then cover it with Karo white syrup and pecan halves. Place rounds of dough, cut side down, on the Karo/pecan mixture. Bake these at 350° until brown and center rolls appear cooked. Be sure to turn out of the pan immediately, while still warm. Cold cooked syrup turns to concrete. Rinse the pan immediately with very hot water.

Finally, to make a round coffee cake, repeat instructions about rolling out dough, dabbing with butter, sprinkling with cinnamon and brown sugar, and rolling it up. Twist into a circle and slash with knife periodically along top to give the dough room to expand. Bake at 350° until done—once again, watch that it doesn't remain doughy in the thickest part.

Once, in a fit of confusion, I made the everlasting rolls recipe into loaves of bread. It was good, but a bit sweet. Mom had a great bread recipe. It doesn't work too well for sandwiches, but it makes the best toast in the world.

ALICE MACBAIN'S WHITE BREAD
    2 pkgs. dry yeast
    ½ c. lukewarm water
    Pinch of sugar
    4 c. milk (1 12-oz. can evaporated milk plus enough water to make 4 cups)
    4 Tbsp. sugar
    4 tsp. salt
    5 Tbsp. oil (scant)
    About 12 c. flour
    Note: If you use fresh milk, you have to scald it or it will kill the yeast. This is too much trouble. Use the canned milk.
    Sprinkle the yeast on a little bit of water and add ½ tsp. sugar to hasten the action—let it rise a bit. Separately mix milk, sugar, salt, oil, and some flour. Add yeast. Add rest of flour. Don't use too much flour—the dough should not be stiff.
    Knead until smooth (5 to 10 minutes). Put into two loaf pans (don't grease the sides or the bread won't rise as well while it bakes). Bake at 400° for 10 minutes, lower to 350°, and bake for 35 to 40 minutes.

Intimidated by kneading dough? Don't be. It's the most calming thing you can do. You can either knead on a large cutting board or in a large bowl—I like bowls. You sort of work the bowl in a circular motion as you turn the dough.

I particularly liked fruit bread that Mom used to make occasionally.

FRUIT LOAF
⅓ c. shortening
⅓ c. dark brown sugar
2 Tbsp. grated lemon peel
2 Tbsp. grated orange peel
1 egg unbeaten
1 c. cottage cheese
1½ c. sifted flour
1½ tsp. baking powder
½ tsp. soda
½ tsp. salt
½ c. each dried prunes and apricots, chopped
Cream the shortening, sugar, and rinds. Add egg. Beat well. Add cheese. Sift dry ingredients and add to first mixture with fruits. Mix well and pack in greased loaf pan. Bake at 350° for 1 hour.

And cookies! The cookies jar was always full when we came home from school, though Mom could hear the clink of the lid against the jar from the other end of the house if one of us was trying to sneak a cookie too close to dinner. I imagine her chocolate chip cookie recipe is pretty much standard, though the addition of soda in hot water probably isn't done much today.

CHOCOLATE CHIP COOKIES

1 c. butter

¾ cup brown sugar

¾ cup white sugar

2 eggs beaten

1 tsp. soda

1 Tbsp. hot water

2¼ c. flour

1 tsp. salt

1 c. chopped nuts (optional)

1 12-oz. pkg. semisweet chocolate bits

1 tsp. vanilla

Cream butter and sugars; add eggs and beat. Dissolve soda in hot water and mix into butter/sugar/egg mixture alternately with flour sifted with the salt. Add chopped nuts (I never do that), chocolate chips, and vanilla. Drop by teaspoonfuls on greased cookie sheet. Bake at 375°—probably about 10 minutes—until edges just begin to brown.

PEANUT BUTTER COOKIES

1 c. brown sugar

¾ c. white sugar

1 c. butter

2 eggs

1 c. smooth peanut butter

2¾ c. flour

2 level tsp. baking soda

½ tsp. salt

Cream sugar and butter. Add eggs and peanut butter. Add flour, soda, and salt. Roll small amount of dough in palm of hand to form a ball. Flatten and pat down with a fork, first one way and then another, so there is a crisscross pattern. Bake at 375° for 10 minutes or until edges barely start to brown.

MOLASSES SUGAR COOKIES

¾ c. shortening

1 c. sugar

¼ c. dark molasses

1 egg

2 tsp. baking soda

2 c. sifted flour

½ tsp. ginger

½ tsp. ground cloves

1 tsp. cinnamon

1 tsp. salt

Melt shortening over low heat. Remove from heat and let cool. Add sugar, molasses, and egg. Beat well. Sift together flour, soda, cloves, ginger, cinnamon, and salt. Add to first mixture. Mix well. Chill at least 30 minutes. Form into one-inch balls, roll in granulated sugar, and place 2 inches apart on greased cookie sheet. Bake in moderately hot oven (375°) for 8-10 minutes. Cookies will flatten out and spread during baking.

Bobby Fantl lived down the block, and he and my brother were great friends. His mother's fudge cookies were unbeatable.

MRS. FANTL'S FUDGE COOKIES

2 oz. bitter chocolate

¼ lb. butter

2 eggs

1 c. sugar

¾ c. flour

1 tsp. vanilla

Melt chocolate and butter. Add remaining ingredients and stir. There's no temperature indication, but I'd guess 350°. There is, however, a strong warning with the recipe: do not bake too long—not more than 20 minutes in a moderate oven. Sprinkle with powdered sugar. Enjoy!

I went to Cornell College in the tiny town of Mount Vernon, Iowa. It wasn't a match for this city girl, and I came home after two years. I learned one important thing in Iowa: a turkey and blue cheese sandwich with mayonnaise is delicious. It's still one of my favorite sandwiches today.

I went back to work for my dad at the hospital, as I'd done in high school, and attended the University of Chicago. An embarrassing admission for an author, but I had to retake freshman English because I had passed out of it at Cornell but did not do so at the U. of C. I graduated with a degree in English but did so poorly on the exit exam that I was told I could never earn a Ph.D. And I kept working at the hospital. Today, friends and colleagues call me one of the most efficient people they've ever met—I learned that from my dad and his administrative assistant. And I always said I had to work harder because I was the boss's daughter.

In spite of a broken heart over the one true love that didn't work out, I was comfortable living at home. Truth is, I didn't know what to do next or differently—and I wasn't, as I've said, adventuresome. But my brother came home on a visit from Kirksville, Missouri, where he was finishing his undergraduate work at the teachers' college so he could attend the Kirksville College of Osteopathic Medicine. He announced in no uncertain terms that I had to get away from home.

And so I moved to another small town and went back to school, this time studying for a master's and working at the osteopathic college. It was my first job in publishing: I was assistant editor of a monthly medical journal, and for a long time I thought medical writing was my calling. I also edited the alumni publication, including doing the old-fashioned paste-up. I didn't know it, but I was beginning to find my career. And I met Joel.

Today, I love to cook, and I'm an experimenter in the kitchen, never afraid to try a new recipe on guests. I once met a high-society lady who always had her cook try out recipes before serving them to guests. Not me—I rush right in with a certain bravado that I don't always show in other parts of my life! I attribute my interest in food and my love of cooking to my mom. It may have been a beef-and-potatoes household, but I learned a lot from her and, best of all, acquired a spirit of adventure in cooking.

Chapter II

Marriage and Two New Worlds of Food

Marriage and a move to Texas brought me two new worlds of food—Jewish cooking and Tex-Mex. I first moved to Kirksville, Missouri, to earn a master's degree, because my brother was in osteopathic medical school there.

Kirksville was better than Mount Vernon. At first, I lived with John and his first wife, Barbara. She was a native of Texas, which at that time was like a foreign country to me. Barbara immediately opened my eyes to new foods, though I remember only one or two things. One was jalapeno chilies, which provided evening entertainment occasionally—who could sit at the kitchen table and eat the most pickled chilies without blanching? I never tried, but I remember Joel ate them almost casually.

Two of Barbara's dishes stand out in my mind, including one that I've never been able to duplicate. She used to caramelize sauerkraut (that stuff I'd never eaten). Barbara would melt butter in the skillet, dump in well-drained kraut, and sauté it, constantly stirring and sprinkling sugar over it, until the kraut was caramelized. It was delicious, and I keep meaning to try it. My brother and I have talked about it, and all we conclude is that it can't be hard to do. But we never do it.

The other was meatless spaghetti, which Barbara claimed she invented one night before they married when John was coming for dinner and she had no money for groceries. She used what she had on hand, melting butter in the skillet, adding cooked spaghetti and lots of lemon juice. I "improved" on the idea by using spinach noodles and adding scallions and mushrooms. Now I also add chopped artichoke hearts and a frozen "ice cube" of homemade pesto. I frequently served "green noodles" as my children were growing up. The dish was a household favorite.

GREEN NOODLES

1 16-0z. pkg. spinach egg noodles

1 stick butter

8 oz. mushrooms, sliced (I always buy whole and slice them myself)

4 scallions, chopped

1 can quartered artichoke hearts

1 ice-cube size piece of pesto, thawed

Juice of one lemon

Grated fresh Parmesan

Cook and drain noodles. Melt butter in the skillet. (Megan, weight-conscious in high school, used to insist that was too much butter, and it may be.) Sauté the mushrooms and scallions in the butter. Add lemon juice to taste—I like lots; the mushrooms soak up the lemon and are delicious. Add noodles and toss to coat. Top with Parmesan

Jamie's wife, Melanie, does a slightly different version for her daughters, Maddie and Edie, both of whom at a very young age love sour things like pickles and capers. Mel cooks angel hair pasta and butters it liberally; then she adds lemon juice and capers. I watched in amazement as she dumped capers in out of the jar, not bothering to drain them (as I always do, with some difficulty). "Oh, yeah," she said, "the juice adds a really good taste." I tried it, and she's right.

In 1964, I married Joel Alter, born and raised in the Bronx, Jewish by heritage but not by active practice. He was attending the osteopathic college, a year ahead of John. He graduated in 1964 but did his internship in Kirksville. For a girl raised in Chicago who had always followed the

The kids took cookie making very seriously.

rules and done what was expected, Joel was a shock. He cared little about manners and convention, yet he talked about books with me endlessly. He lived in a pigpen, but I found that charming. To my horror, he dumped all his laundry—rugs, bed linens, dish towels, and underwear—into one oversize load. Somehow I remember that most clearly. He told wild stories about his youth—how he had trained guard dogs for Macy's Department Store and similar things—stories that I later doubted were true. But he was the only man who made me comfortable on the dance floor, and I fell head over heels.

We married, against my parents' wishes, in my brother's backyard (next to a goat pen) with a Church of Christ minister officiating—something I find particularly ironic since he was uniting a Jew and a Methodist, but he was a good friend. We lived in a house almost in the country that was built by adding various rooms to an old hunting cabin. Each room was a different level, and I joked that I lived in a split-level home. We had dogs (lots of them), a mailbox that read, "Alters' Ego," and a lot of friends in Kirksville. I used to think I wanted to live in that house forever. A year after we moved to Texas, I went back to Kirksville and was amazed at how stifling the social life was.

In 1965, we moved to Fort Worth so that Joel could take a surgical residency. I still didn't know what I wanted to be when I grew up, so I began work on a Ph.D. in English at TCU. They thought I was a prize catch because I came from the University of Chicago—introducing me, the chair of the department would always skip lightly over my years in Missouri. I got an NDEA (National Defense Education Act) fellowship and was earning almost as much as I had during my brief stint as a pathology secretary.

Anne holding the newest baby, either Jamie or Jordan (they both had dark hair). I think this is Jordan.

I had lived in a predominantly Jewish neighborhood in Chicago, and I remember walking by the deli that was next to the movie theater. I always thought of it as a mysterious place, full of strange foods that I would never eat—rolls of sausage hung by strings from hooks and trays of dried fish in the window. This was too strange for a child from a meat-and-potatoes household.

Joel introduced me to those foods, and I love most of them still today—though Joel and I have long since gone our separate ways, bound only by our children.

The first thing I learned to eat was lox and bagels—maybe a natural, given my fondness for fish. Lox is not smoked salmon—it is salt-cured. Ideally, it is eaten for Sunday morning brunch on a bagel lavishly spread with cream cheese. (True deli cream cheese is richer and better by far than the commercial brands to which we are all accustomed.) Then it is topped with a slice of onion and a slice of tomato. I am not a bread eater, and because bagels are a lot of bread and make a really thick sandwich to bite into, these days I prefer my lox and cream cheese on rye toast. Our local deli,

Carshon's, is no longer open on Sundays—a travesty—so I sometimes treat myself to a lox lunch during the week. And Colin, my oldest son, doesn't think a visit back home is complete without a trip to Carshon's.

I recently also rediscovered an old favorite at Carshon's, a breakfast dish that Joel used to cook: lox and eggs. He simply put diced lox into eggs as he scrambled them. I once saw a recipe for "Lox and Eggs Elegante"; the name was enough to set me giggling, let alone the fact that it included mushrooms, green pepper (which I can't abide), and basil. Gilding the lily!

LOX AND EGGS

1 scallion, chopped
2 Tbsp. butter
½ lb. lox, chopped
6 eggs
2 Tbsp. milk

Sauté onion in butter, add diced lox, and then fold in eggs and milk. Cook and stir until desired consistency.
Optional: add diced tomatoes.

Joel also cooked salami and eggs, and not long ago I took Colin's wife, Lisa, to Carshon's for breakfast. Lisa, not a fish eater, did not want lox, but she ordered salami and eggs and was astounded when the salami was cut up and scrambled into the eggs. "I expected some sliced salami on the side," she said, but she loved it and wants to go back for more.

SALAMI AND EGGS

Follow the recipe for lox and eggs, substituting ½ lb. salami for the lox.

Joel's mother, Grandma Bernice, came to visit occasionally after she was widowed. She used to drive me crazy, asking things like, "Judy, dear, is this the way you chop an onion?" I wanted to shout, "You've been cooking a lot longer than I have! Just chop the blasted onion!" But I refrained.

Bernice was strictly an "old country" cook—and diner. We once took her to an upscale restaurant and ordered vichyssoise. She hesitated, spoon poised over the soup while she looked questioningly at her son. "You know, Ma," he said reassuringly, "vichyssoise, like cold potato soup."

She shuddered with horror. "Cold potato soup? I couldn't eat it." And there was a wasted cup of vichyssoise.

But my goodness, could she do a brisket that was delicious and bore no relation to Texas barbecued brisket! She said you had to ask the butcher for first-cut breast, which Joel tried to tell me was the "hangy-down thing" at a cow's neck. I knew he was wrong. I was also amused at the thought of what a Texas butcher would say if I asked for first-cut breast.

BERNICE'S BRISKET

Brisket

Salt, pepper, onion or garlic powder, paprika

2 onions, sliced

The night before cooking, season brisket with salt, pepper, onion or garlic powder, and paprika (Bernice pronounced it "pa-pree-káh," with the emphasis on the last syllable). Refrigerate.

Next day, slice the onions. Brown the brisket in a heavy skillet; then cover it with sliced onions, add water, cover, and simmer all day, adding water as needed. Serve with kasha and bow tie noodles.

Ah, kasha. That's another story. Kasha is roasted buckwheat groats. In Russia, where Bernice came from at the age of eleven, it could have meant a variety of grains. Joel loved it with bow ties, but I found it tasteless. I did find a recipe I liked.

KASHA MY WAY

1 egg beaten

1 c. uncooked kasha

1½ tsp. salt

1½ tsp. marjoram

1/2 c. butter or margarine, divided use

2½ c. boiling water

2 c. sliced mushrooms

1 onion sliced

½ c. sour cream

Mix egg into kasha in a small bowl. Put egg/kasha mixture in a large, heavy skillet and heat until dry, stirring all the time. Add salt, thyme, marjoram and ¼ cup butter. Add 2 cups boiling water. Stir thoroughly, cover, and simmer half an hour.

In another pan, sauté mushrooms, celery, and onion in remaining butter until soft. Add to kasha, along with final ½ cup boiling water. Only add the water if the kasha is too dry. Simmer 10 minutes.

Just before serving, place it in a serving dish and top with dollops of sour cream. (The sour cream is essential! Don't leave it out.)

Bernice also made us kugel, a pudding of either potatoes or noodles with eggs. Generally it is an accompaniment to meat, but a sweet noodle kugel—with cinnamon and raisins—is sometimes served for dessert.

Occasionally, Bernice made kreplach—little meat dumplings. But truthfully I prefer Natchitoches meat pies (as in Natchitoches, Louisiana). For several years I taught a noncredit creative writing class at TCU. One semester, the class really "bonded"—a term I use with some caution—and the final class session was a potluck supper at my home. One man, husband of a TCU colleague, brought these meat pies.

NATCHITOCHES MEAT PIES

Filling:

1½ lbs. ground beef

1½ lbs. ground pork

1 c. chopped green onions, tops and bottoms

1 Tbsp. salt

1 tsp. course [sic] ground black pepper

1 tsp. coarse ground red pepper

½ tsp. cayenne pepper

⅓ cup flour

Crust:

2 c. self-rising flour

⅓ heaping c. Crisco, not melted

1 egg, beaten

¾ c. milk

Combine all filling ingredients except the flour and cook until meat loses its red color. Do NOT overcook. Sift the flour over the meat (does anyone sift anymore?) and stir frequently. Cool to room temperature. Drain in colander to remove grease and juice.

For crust, sift flour and cut shortening into it. Add beaten egg and milk. Form dough into a ball and roll out about one-third of it on lightly floured board or pastry cloth. Cut into 5-inch circles.

Place a heaping Tbsp. of filling on one side of the pastry circle. Dampen the edge of the pie with fingertips, fold dough over the meat, and crimp with fork. Prick top with fork.

Fry in deep-fat fryer at 350° until golden brown.

Uncooked, these freeze nicely in sandwich bags. Do not thaw frozen pies before cooking. For cocktail pies, use a biscuit cutter and 1 tsp. of filling.

Helpful hint: I found I always had more filling than dough, and the dough was difficult to work with. I use Pillsbury crescent rolls, rolled thin. This is much easier and still good.

Joel badly wanted children, though I had never given the idea much thought. I suppose I thought children would just naturally come along—but they didn't. Every month was a major disappointment, and I knew he was frustrated. We adopted four children, in an era when adoption agencies said to you, "If you have one child, we will help you complete your family; if you have two, your family is complete." Our oldest children, Colin and Megan, are clones of my northern European heritage. Colin is half German, half Scotch-Irish—my exact background. Megan has a little French thrown in. Jamie is half Greek and half Chinese, and the agency promised us a dark-haired child to "balance" our family. When Jamie was three, they called about Jordan, who is supposedly half Mexican Indian. None of us can see it. Her dark hair curls, and her skin is fair.

People sometimes ask when we told the children that they were adopted. What's to tell? The older three knew that babies came from the adoption agency because they always went with us to pick up the next baby. I guess Jordan just picked it up. But there was never that "moment of great revelation."

Dinnertime was a family affair. This was before Jordan was born.

I loved the years of babies and toddlers and often long for them today. With grandchildren, it's not quite the same. They love you, but you're not the first person they turn to. But I have to admit that when my children were little, I had a housekeeper who took charge from 9 A.M. until 4 P.M. I retreated to my office and wrote. Some days I thought, "I'd write, if I knew what to write." But I did articles for a national osteopathic health publication for lay readers on topics such as "Tell me, doctor, if I have a pain in my side, is it appendicitis?" And I once got a small piece on adoption into *McCall's*, perhaps the zenith of my magazine career.

Then, in 1978, I wrote my first novel. I didn't intend to write a young-adult novel, but the agent I was using sold it as such, and suddenly I was categorized as a young-adult author. It's an identity that has stuck with me all these years, even though I've written quite a bit for adults. But it's also an identity that has brought me a lot of freelance work. Suddenly, I was writing books—not a lot of them, not often, but I was writing.

Joel and I agreed to raise our children in both the Protestant and Jewish faiths, although he did not practice his faith, and during the marriage I wasn't very faithful to mine. But we celebrated the high holy days of both.

For Christmas, we celebrated much as my family did, usually with my parents, serving turkey and all the trimmings. Easter was more experimental, but usually the main course was ham. I would have served lamb, but Jamie, the best eater among my children, dislikes it, and I figured he was entitled to dislike a few things. He and Mel won't eat mushrooms either—it's the texture thing.

We also had Hanukkah dinners and seders during Passover, although one half-Jewish friend said after a seder at our house that he'd never been to a seder before and had a sneaky feeling he still hadn't been. But we did try to follow tradition.

We always shared Hanukkah with the family of a fellow English graduate student. We made latkes (potato pancakes), which we served with the requisite sour cream and applesauce. For some bizarre reason, we usually followed them with egg salad and tuna salad. The mom in that household always brought her parents, and her dad carried a fat roll of dollar bills, which he peeled off, giving one to each child. They were thrilled.

LATKES

   1 lb. baking potatoes
   ½ c. chopped onion
   1 egg
   Salt

Coarsely grate the potatoes with an old-fashioned grater. (Do not use a food processor.) As you grate each batch, put in cold water. When all potatoes are grated, drain in colander; then roll in towel to squeeze out every bit of water. Put in a bowl and add salt and egg. Drop spoonfuls in hot (but not smoking) vegetable oil (they will flatten) and fry until brown; turn and brown other side. Keep cooked latkes warm in oven, in layers of paper towels to drain the grease, while you cook the others. Best if served immediately after cooked. This makes about fifteen latkes.

For seders, we'd cook and serve the traditional food, including gefilte fish with red horseradish. Gefilte fish cakes are made of ground whitefish or carp, eggs, matzo meal, and seasonings and then simmered in vegetable broth. We bought them in jars, but many older Jewish families made their own. I always remember a high school classmate whose mother, called to the phone, asked her to stir the gefilte fish on the stove. The girl, whose name escapes me though I can see her face, was doing laundry and had a box of detergent in her hand. Somehow the detergent ended up in the fish broth, and she was afraid to tell her mother because of the cost of the ingredients. She held her breath when the fish was served, but no one noticed a thing.

Jamie particularly liked gefilte fish, so a few years ago I bought a jar for him to add to his Easter dinner; he tasted it, looked at me, and said, "It doesn't taste like it did when I was a kid."

We also tried to be traditional, serving foods that fit dietary restrictions—no leavened bread. But no remarkable recipes came out of those evenings, just wonderful memories: Colin, my oldest son, opening the door for Elijah, everyone drinking too much of the terribly sweet Mogen David wine, monumental piles of dishes to wash after all those courses.

Joel was, at that time, more sophisticated about some foods than I was. He introduced me to oysters and cherrystone clams on the half shell, escargot—I didn't much like the snails themselves, but I loved to sop up the sauce with slices of French bread—and caviar. He could eat more caviar than any person I've met.

Another thing I learned to love—and still eat, sparingly, to this day—is chopped chicken liver. After we got to Texas, Joel had a patient whose wife made chopped liver which he brought to us once a week; —I have never since tasted it better. But Ben Rausch, who brought it to us, is long gone from memory, as are all those days.

These days I eat my chopped liver at Carshon's. Mary, the manager, graciously agreed to share her recipe. She does all the major cooking there, from chopped liver and potato salad to heavenly chocolate meringue pies.

She gave me, however, restaurant-size quantities. I divided it roughly by one-third.

CARSHON'S CHOPPED LIVER

1 lb. chicken livers

1 large onion, sliced

6 eggs, hard-boiled

Rendered chicken fat (sold in delicatessens as "schmalz" and very tasty, but oh! not good for you)

Cook the livers in a small amount of chicken fat. Remove from the pan and wash the pan. Add chicken fat and heat; when hot, add onion. Brown the onion. Add precooked livers on top of onions. Season with salt and pepper. Reduce heat, cover, and cook slowly. Remove cover and raise heat to evaporate the liquid. Grind livers and onion with hard-boiled eggs.

Instead of grinding, when I used to make chopped liver, I used a wooden chopping bowl and chopper. Grandma Bernice gave me one that I had for years until the bowl cracked into two pieces. I'm still looking for another. The chopper is a rounded blade with a handle. You simply chop the liver and eggs until it's as pulverized as if you'd put it in a grinder. Great served with bagel chips or in a rye-bread sandwich.

You can also make great egg salad in a chopping bowl.

I swear I had never had Mexican or Tex-Mex food until I moved to Texas. In college I spent a summer in Albuquerque, staying with a friend's family and taking classes at the University of New Mexico. I distinctly remember a day trip to Taos and a small diner on the plaza (I think I've seen the same place in recent years). Everyone ordered Mexican food—which is very different in New Mexico from what you find in Texas—and I staunchly had a BLT.

I suppose my first introduction to Tex-Mex was at Fort Worth's famed Joe T. Garcia's restaurant. We went to professional meetings there, and I slowly learned to eat cheese enchiladas, tacos, and guacamole. To this day I scrape the chilies off the wonderful cheese nachos they serve as an appetizer. But the thing I loved best—and still do—is the beans. Rumor is that at Joe T.'s the beans are "boracchio," made with beer. I know they're also made with lard and are as bad for you as chopped liver, but I do like them.

My mother cooked "northern" or "sweet" beans—navy beans from the can that she doctored with molasses or brown sugar, mustard, ketchup, and onion. I used to do that, too, until I discovered Bush's original beans. They honestly do taste just like those Mom made and are a lot easier. But I had never seen a pinto bean.

Soon, though, Joel and I were serving brisket and beans. He'd rub the brisket with an equal mixture of salt, pepper, paprika, and sugar and slow-cook it all day in a covered grill—heat at one end of the grill and the meat at the other.

I also had a good oven barbecue recipe. After Joel went into practice, his partners would have an annual Christmas family dinner, with a standardized menu. One year it was barbecue, and I got this recipe:

OVEN BARBECUE
  Brisket
  Figaro liquid smoke
  Worcestershire sauce
  Salt and pepper
  Garlic powder
  Celery salt
  Night before: sprinkle Figaro liquid smoke liberally on both sides of a
  brisket of whatever size will fit in your largest pan (use the entire 4 oz.
  bottle); cover both sides with onion powder, garlic powder, and celery
  salt. Cover and refrigerate.
  Next day: cover both sides with Worcestershire, salt, and pepper.
  Cover and cook, fat side down, for 6 hours or more in a 275° oven.
  Pour off fat and juices (or most of them) and cover meat with commercial barbecue sauce. Cook for one hour more.

HOMEMADE BARBECUE SAUCE (to be served with the meat)

    1 lg. bottle ketchup (26 oz.)

    Ketchup bottle ¾ full of water

    1 medium onion, chopped

    3 cloves garlic, chopped

    Bring this to a boil, reduce to simmer and add:

    Salt and pepper

    1 tsp. paprika

    1 tsp. cayenne

    3 Tbsp. Worcestershire

    Juice of one lemon

    1 or 2 tsp. brown sugar

    1 tsp. dried mustard

    Simmer 1 hour; then melt a stick of butter in it.

You have to serve barbecued brisket with beans. This is the best pinto bean recipe I've ever found.

PLAIN BUT GOOD PINTO BEANS

    1 lb. pinto beans

    Water to cover

    1 large onion, diced

    Small piece of salt pork, diced

    5 bouillon cubes

    Wash beans and sort, throwing away split ones and wrinkled, shriveled ones. Cover with cold water and soak overnight. In the morning, dice onion and salt pork and sauté. Drain beans and cover with fresh water. Add sautéed onion and salt pork and bouillon cubes. Simmer all day. (The bouillon cubes make all the difference with these beans.)

You might want to serve the world's easiest marinated vegetables with this barbecue and beans. My kids still ask for this today, and Megan often keeps a batch in her refrigerator.

MARINATED VEGETABLE SALAD

1 small head broccoli

1 small cauliflower, cut into flowerets

2 or 3 cans cut green beans (not French cut)

1 can quartered artichoke hearts

1 red onion, sliced thin

8 oz. mushrooms, sliced

1 large bottle commercial Italian salad dressing

Blanch broccoli and cauliflower and cut into bite-sized pieces. Cool quickly with ice or cold water so they don't get mushy. Mix with canned green beans, sliced onions, mushrooms, and canned artichoke hearts. (The original recipe calls for an avocado and leaf lettuce, but I think avocados get lost and the lettuce gets soggy.) Pour Italian salad dressing over it and refrigerate until it's cold.

Megan recently gave me a recipe that's sort of a variation of this. Its Texas caviar, of which there are a thousand varieties, but this is her version, which her son Sawyer loves. (I'd cut back on chiles and Tabasco and omit the green pepper, but that's me.)

TEXAS CAVIAR

3 16-oz. cans black-eyed peas, drained and rinsed of all juice

1 bunch scallions, thinly sliced, green part only

1 Tbsp. fresh oregano

1 Tbsp. Tabasco

1 Tbsp. Worcestershire

1 tsp. black pepper

½ bunch parsley, chopped

3 canned or fresh jalapeno chilies, chopped

1 firm, ripe tomato, chopped

2 cups vinaigrette

1 green bell pepper, chopped

3 cloves garlic, pressed or minced

Mix and refrigerate for 4 to 6 hours. The longer it sits, the better it is.

At the Texas College of Osteopathic Medicine, Joel taught with a physiologist named Bob Kaman. His wife was Suzi, and we saw them occasionally socially. I probably haven't seen Suzi Kaman in thirty years and never did know her well, but my family has enjoyed her bean salad over and over.

SUZI KAMAN'S BEAN SALAD

1 large can Ranch Style beans, drained and rinsed

1 onion chopped

1 tomato chopped, or more if you want

Grated cheese to taste

At least 1 4-oz. can chopped green chilies

Chopped lettuce (I found it got soggy and usually left it out)

Fritos

1 small bottle Catalina dressing

Mix all together and chill. Helpful hint: I often omitted or cut down the Catalina—everything else had such good flavors! And I learned to serve the Fritos on the side, so that they stayed crisp. If you put them in the salad and you have leftovers, the chips get soggy and awful and nobody will eat the leftovers.

Years later, I found a stewed bean recipe that I think is great.

STEWED BEANS

Cook one slice bacon until crisp.

In same skillet, pour off all but 1 Tbsp. drippings.

Add:

½ c. chopped onion

1 medium carrot, diced

¼ tsp. salt

¼ tsp. pepper

¼ tsp. thyme

Cook, stirring, until onion is tender. Then add:

1 Tbsp. tomato puree

1 14½-oz. can diced stewed tomatoes

1 16-oz. can pinto beans, unflavored, drained

2 Tbsp. chopped parsley

2 Tbsp. red wine vinegar

Crumble bacon into pan and simmer. Makes six servings. Enough of beans.

Joel's partners' wives and I also cooked lasagna for one of our Christmas dinners—white lasagna.

WHITE LASAGNA

8 oz. lasagna noodles

1 lb. ground beef

1 c. finely chopped celery

½ c. finely chopped onion

1 clove garlic, crushed

2 tsp. dried powdered basil

1 tsp. dried oregano

¾ tsp. salt and ¼ tsp. pepper

½ tsp. Italian herb seasoning

1 c. light cream

1 3-oz. pkg. cream cheese, cubed

½ c. dry white wine

2 c. shredded cheddar

1½ c. shredded Gouda cheese (or use all cheddar, depending on your taste)

1 12-oz. carton creamy cottage cheese

1 slightly beaten egg

12 oz. mozzarella, sliced

Cook lasagna noodles and drain. Set aside. (Of course, today they have noodles you don't have to pre-cook; it's been a long time since I made lasagna, so I'm not sure about those.)

In skillet, brown beef, celery, onion and garlic until meat is brown and vegetables are soft. Drain excess fat. Stir in basil, oregano, salt, ½ tsp. pepper, and Italian herb seasoning. Add cream and cream cheese. Cook and stir over low heat until cream cheese melts. Stir in wine. Gradually stir in Gouda and cheddar

Separately stir together cottage cheese and egg.

Layer half noodles in greased 13x9 pan; top with half meat sauce, half cottage cheese, and half mozzarella. Repeat layers. Bake covered for 30 to 35 minutes at 375°. Let stand 10 minutes before serving. Serves twelve generously.

Early in our marriage, Joel and I discovered that we liked to entertain and to cook together, although too often he cooked (flamboyantly, for an audience) and I found myself alone in the kitchen at midnight, washing dishes. Still we developed a reputation as adventuresome and good cooks, and we enjoyed it.

One of our earliest adventures, when we were penniless (he a resident and I was a graduate student) was a "bring your own lobster" party. A local seafood restaurant/market once a year had a "two for one" lobster sale.

Sunday night dinner at Mom's house.

We borrowed a huge pot from the hospital kitchen for boiling the lobsters, I made a large salad, and each couple brought their own wine (in those days it may have been Mateus). We boiled the lobsters and served them with lots of lemon and butter. I've heard much today about the cruelty of boiling live lobsters, but I can't help myself—I love them!

We also developed the tradition of tree-trimming parties. When I was a child, trimming the Christmas tree was an ordeal. My parents and I went to buy the tree—not too much trauma there—and my father and my brother put it up and put the lights on, never with a spirit of festivity. Then they decamped, and Mom and I decorated it. I always thought decorating the tree should be a festive affair, so the first year we married Joel and I invited friends to help. For years, we tended to serve the same thing year after year.

A recipe I used at the very first tree trimming and still use occasionally:

CHILI CHEESE DIP

Mix 2 large cans Wolf Brand chili without beans and 1 large Velveeta brick. Heat thoroughly and serve with tortilla chips. It's still great, all these years later. I recently went to a church chili cook-off and the Cub Scouts had fixed the very same recipe.

Another version adds picante and sausage. This is Colin's favorite dip, and I sometimes served it to the children as a main dish, because it's so hearty. The nice thing about this is you can make it mild or hot, depending on what kind of sausage and what strength picante sauce you choose. I usually went middle of the road. For supper, serve it in bowls, with a bowl of tortilla chips, and a green salad. As an appetizer, serve it in the crockpot with a bowl of tortilla chips on the side.

COLIN'S QUESO

1 lb. hamburger
1 lb. sausage
1 lb. Velveeta
1 can mushroom soup
1 jar Pace picante sauce

Brown hamburger and sausage, breaking up the chunks of meat until it is all crumbly. Drain and put in the crockpot. Add Velveeta, cut in chunks, and melt. Add mushroom soup and picante sauce (really works best if you use Pace).

One year I didn't cook for tree trimming—I can't remember the circumstances, but I know we made it a dessert party and hired a caterer. It was on Sunday night, so the children, after being paraded before guests to say hello, went to their bedrooms and put on PJs. The caterer thought he'd give them a treat and took small servings of chocolate mousse to them. "Look, kids, chocolate pudding!"

They tasted it and almost in chorus said scornfully, "That's not pudding. It's mousse!"

We had raised young sophisticates.

Today, I send out invitations most years to "Judy Alter's almost annual tree-trimming party." Sometimes there's a tree, but most often there's not, because I'm planning to be out of town for Christmas, either in Santa Fe with all my family or visiting at one of their homes. The menu has changed over the years, and yet it hasn't. I always serve the cheese ball from my childhood Christmas Eve suppers. Some years past I used to serve a huge bowl of pickled herring, with small party ryes, but these days I may be the only one among my friends who likes herring. I've served pork tenderloin with a variety of mustards and mini buns. I've served smoked salmon (when feeling flush) and smoked turkey sandwiches. And I almost always serve something with caviar.

This is my favorite caviar appetizer.

CAVIAR SPREAD
　　2 8-oz. pkg. cream cheese, softened
　　1 3-oz. pkg. cream cheese, softened
　　1 c. mayonnaise
　　1 small onion, grated
　　 1 Tbsp. Worcestershire
　　1 Tbsp. lemon juice
　　Dash of hot sauce
　　1 4-oz. jar black caviar
　　3-4 hard-cooked eggs, finely chopped
　　Chopped parsley

Mix first seven ingredients with electric mixer until smooth. Spoon into shallow serving dish. Top with caviar, eggs, and parsley. Serve with small pumpernickel breads.

I used to make a layered caviar spread that is really good but a lot more work.

LAYERED CAVIAR SPREAD
First layer:
6 hard-boiled eggs, sieved
8 Tbsp. melted butter
1 Tbsp. grated onion
Second layer:
4 Tbsp. mayonnaise
4 tsp. anchovy paste
Chopped parsley
Mix and spread thinly on top of first layer. Refrigerate until set.
Third layer:
4 oz. black caviar
2 Tbsp. grated onion
1 Tbsp. lemon juice
Mix and spread on top of second layer. Chill thoroughly. It may seep a little liquid; mop it up with a paper towel.
When you serve it, you can decorate with sour cream if you wish.

And yet another caviar dish. I remember serving this to a crowd at Thanksgiving that included a man I was dating (after I was divorced), and I think this dip and that dinner were what captivated him.

ARTICHOKE HEARTS WITH CAVIAR
1 8-oz. pkg. cream cheese, softened
1 Tbsp. sour cream
2 tsp. mayonnaise

1 tsp. lemon juice

1 can artichoke hearts, drained and chopped

2 tsp. grated onion

Dash of garlic salt

1 4-oz. jar caviar

Combine ingredients except caviar. Shape into a round mound and flatten enough to spread caviar on top.

My kids all love bourbon hot dogs, another tree-trimming standard.

BOURBON HOT DOGS

2 lbs. hot dogs

¾ c. bourbon

2 c. ketchup

½ c. brown sugar

2 Tbsp. minced onion

Cut hot dogs into half-inch pieces. Combine other ingredients and simmer until sugar melts. Add hot dogs and continue to simmer. Serve warm with toothpicks.

Megan, who will eat anything with jalapenos, likes this spinach-bacon spread.

SPINACH-BACON SPREAD

8 slices bacon, cooked and crumbled

2 10-oz. pkgs. chopped spinach, thawed and well drained

32 oz. Monterey Jack cheese with jalapeños, shredded

1 11-oz. can cheddar cheese soup, undiluted

1 8-oz. pkg. cream cheese

1 tsp. Greek seasoning

½ tsp. onion power

1 tsp. Tabasco

Paprika

1 2-oz. jar diced pimiento, drained (I don't much like pimiento and often leave this out).

Combine everything but bacon, pimiento, and paprika. Heat until cheese melts. Stir in crumbled bacon; sprinkle with pimiento and paprika if you want. Serve hot with crackers.

An easy oldie-but-goodie from friend and fellow publisher Fran Vick:

CRAB AND CREAM CHEESE BRICK

2 8-oz. bricks of cream cheese

Lettuce

6 oz. drained crab meat

About 6-8 oz. chili sauce

Put cream cheese bricks on a bed of lettuce. Cover with drained crab meat. Top with chili sauce. (Be careful not to overdo the chili sauce, or your appetizer will be a mess, difficult to eat.) Serve with crackers.

Jordan's favorite tree trimming recipe:

SMOKY SALMON SPREAD

1 can (14½ oz.) salmon

2 8-oz. pkgs. cream cheese

3 Tbsp. lemon juice

3 Tbsp. sour cream

1½ tsp. dill weed (optional)

¼ cup thinly sliced scallions

3-4 drops hickory liquid smoke

Drain the salmon. Beat the cream cheese and lemon juice and cream together. Add salmon, dill, onions, and liquid smoke. You can use the 7-oz. can of salmon and cut the recipe in half for smaller crowds. One caution: be very careful not to overdo the liquid smoke. Too much ruins the dish.

Potted salmon is another way to serve salmon as an appetizer, without the expense of a whole smoked salmon or some equally showy presentation.

POTTED SALMON

2 14½-oz. cans salmon or 2 lbs. cooked salmon

¼ lb. butter

1 tsp. anchovy paste or chopped anchovies

¼ tsp. mace or nutmeg

¼ tsp. cayenne

1 Tbsp. tarragon vinegar

Freshly ground pepper

Flake drained salmon and process as finely as possible in food processor. Add butter, anchovy, mace or nutmeg, cayenne, vinegar, and pepper. Blend until thoroughly combined and smooth. Spoon into a pan. This will keep in the refrigerator for more than a week if you cover the top entirely with melted butter. Once again, this makes a really big batch and might easily be halved.

When the kids were little, I used to make them mini-pecan rolls. One night I fixed the following appetizer recipe for company and the kids sneaked some, thinking they were pecan rolls. They got what was, for them, an unpleasant surprise.

ANCHOVY ROLLS

1 pkg. crescent rolls

3 Tbsp. anchovy paste (about one tube)

2 Tbsp. butter or margarine, softened

Dash of garlic powder

Unroll the dough on floured surface, pinch the perforations together, and make the dough into four rectangles. Blend anchovy paste, butter, and garlic powder and spread over each of the rectangles. Roll up, beginning at the narrow end. Slice each roll into half-inch pieces. Put on ungreased cookie sheet and bake for 10 to 12 minutes at 350°. Serve hot. Makes about two dozen.

I love goat cheese almost any way you can think to serve it. This recipe is great, though the cheese slices are a little difficult to serve—they fall apart. I may rethink doing this for a large party. If I use it for tree trimming, I double it, although you have to remember that a recipe that serves twenty, as this one does, goes a lot further when you have a whole table full of appetizers and hors d'oeuvres.

MARINATED GOAT CHEESE

1 lb. plain goat cheese

1 Tbsp. fresh rosemary (so easy to grow!)

1 Tbsp. fresh, minced lemon peel

1 garlic clove, minced in a garlic press

¼ tsp. fresh ground pepper

1 c. olive oil

Cut cheese into slices, logs or whatever suits your fancy. Combine everything but the goat cheese. Put the cheese in a dish large enough to accommodate it in a single layer. Pour remaining ingredients over it and refrigerate at least two days. (Five is better.)

Before serving, return cheese to room temperature. Drain by transferring to a platter with a slotted spoon. Drizzle just a little marinade over it. Decorate with something green, like chopped parsley.

SUN-DRIED TOMATO CHEESE SPREAD

1 bulb garlic

1 tsp. olive oil

11 oz. goat cheese

8-oz. pkg. cream cheese

½ c. sun-dried tomatoes packed in oil, drained and chopped

2 Tbsp. chopped chives

¼ tsp. salt

Put the garlic on a strong piece of foil, cut the end off, and drizzle it with oil. Fold the foil over to seal and bake, on a cookie sheet, at 425° for 45 minutes (cloves should be soft and mash easily, after it cools slightly).

Beat garlic and remaining ingredients with mixer until well blended. Chill before serving with crackers, crudités, whatever you want.

Brie is a favorite tree-trimming offering. I used to order it from Carshon's, where Mary puts an apricot filling on Brie *en croute*. Then I discovered a wonderful topping.

BAKED BRIE WITH BROWN SUGAR TOPPING

1 8-inch wheel Brie

1 c. dark brown sugar

1 tsp. cayenne

Mix sugar and cayenne and spread on Brie after removing top white rind. (Do not remove rind from sides or the cheese will run all over the plate it cooks on.) Bake at 350° until topping melts a bit and cheese is softened.

I found this topping in a recipe for Tesuque tortillas (Tesuque is a charming small village outside Santa Fe):

12 flour tortillas

Butter

Brown sugar mixture

Butter tortillas, sprinkle with sugar mixture, cut in strips, and bake at 450° for five minutes. Good as an appetizer or an accompaniment for after-dinner coffee if you aren't serving dessert.

In the late '90s, Colin managed a small diving hotel on Grand Cayman Island. He had a Jamaican cook who fixed the best stuffed mushrooms I've ever eaten. The most I was able to get out of Colin was that the stuffing had shredded yellow cheese (I always believe sharp is best).

CRAB-STUFFED MUSHROOMS

Cream cheese

Shredded sharp cheddar

White wine

Crab meat

Worcestershire sauce

Garlic or garlic butter

You're on your own with proportions, but do bake the mushrooms until they are soft; then, if necessary, broil them briefly.

During those years of cooking gourmet dinners and feeding little children, a friend named Anne Perkins (now Anne Isham) lived with us briefly. She often fixed oatmeal for the children for breakfast, so much so that Colin said to me one day, "Anne says if you don't eat breakfast, something bad will happen." He paused a long time and then looked seriously at me and said, "What?"

The Alter family in the summer of 1976 at a lake in Missouri.

Anne briefly dated a doctor who had recently been divorced from his second wife. He used to appear at our house occasionally for dinner, and one night he said something flip about knowing what the kitchen was—it was the room between the garage and the living room. Somehow that evolved into the idea of *Single Again! Sam's book of bachelor survival.* We all had a grand time putting that together. Sam—and several other newly divorced men—supplied the things they did and didn't know. One said he slept on one side of the bed one week and the other the next so he didn't have to wash the sheets so often. He also confessed to thinking if a little detergent in the washing machine was good, a lot would be better—disaster, of course, ensued. Anne and I contributed the recipes; Sam didn't really have any. And I edited and wrote the text between recipes.   Recently I heard a radio program about the new *Gourmet* cookbook, and Ruth Reichl, the much-acclaimed editor (whose books I like immensely) talked about a recipe for butter-based salad dressing, which she admitted sounded odd but proclaimed was really wonderful. It made me think of Anne's recipe, which is in Sam's book. I like to think Anne was way ahead of *Gourmet Magazine.*

BUTTER SALAD DRESSING
Juice of one big lemon
½ c. softened butter (1 stick)
2 Tbsp. vinegar
¼ c. salad oil (now I'd probably use olive oil)
⅓ tsp. dried tarragon
1 tsp. dried parsley flakes
½ tsp. lemon pepper
½ tsp. seasoned salt
¼ tsp. dill weed
¼ tsp. black pepper

Anne has now written her own cookbook. A confessed chocoholic, she goes around the country promoting *Eat Chocolate, Lose Weight: The Chocoholic's Survival Guide and Practical Handbook.* She may be the only person in Texas who likes chocolate better than I do, but she is by now pretty fussy about chocolate, scorning the everyday stuff.

Another recipe from Sam's book is one that I used to cook for guests before I developed an allergy to shrimp (I long for this one, too). I used to serve it preceded by vichyssoise (we didn't think about cholesterol in those days):

VICHYSSOISE

1 can cream of potato soup

1 soup can milk

1 Tbsp. minced scallions

1 tsp. Worcestershire

Dash of pepper.

Combine in blender, blend until smooth, and chill.

This was followed by Shrimp Victoria—yikes, when I think of the calories now!

SHRIMP VICTORIA

½ c. minced onion

¼ lb butter (1 stick)

¾ lb. sliced mushrooms

1½ lb. cooked shrimp.

2 Tbsp. flour

1 tsp. salt

Dash of pepper.

2 c. sour cream

Sauté onion in butter. Add mushrooms; cook 2 minutes. Add shrimp. Cook four minutes, stirring; add flour, salt, and pepper. Stir well and keep warm.

Just before serving, stir in sour cream; cook only until hot. Do *not* let it boil. (I'm sure you could reduce the amount of sour cream.)

For some reason I connect the following recipe with Sam. He probably doesn't remember it, but I recently dragged it out and cooked it for a new neighbor, who had high praise for it.

GOUGÈRE WITH HAM AND MUSHROOMS

(The recipe says to make the paté a choux first, but it makes more sense to me to make the filling first and have it ready when you make the puff pastry.)

Filling:

4 Tbsp. butter or margarine

1 medium onion, chopped

½ lb. sliced mushrooms

1½ Tbsp. flour

1 tsp. salt

¼ tsp. pepper

1 tsp. instant chicken broth

1 c. hot water

1 large tomato, peeled, seeded, and quartered

6 oz. cooked ham, cut into thin strips

2 Tbsp. shredded sharp cheddar

2 Tbsp. chopped parsley

Melt butter in skillet; sauté onion until soft—don't let it brown. Add mushrooms and cook two minutes. Sprinkle mixture with flour, salt, and pepper. Stir and cook two minutes. Add chicken broth and water; mix and bring to boil. Simmer briefly. Remove sauce from stove, add ham strips. Cut tomato into quarters and add.

For the paté a choux (cream puff pastry in English, gougère in French):

1 c. sifted flour

Pinch salt and pepper

1 c. water

½ c. butter (one stick)

4 eggs

½ lb. sharp cheddar cheese, diced

Mix flour, salt and pepper, heat water and butter until butter melts. Bring to boiling and dump the flour in all at once. Stir until mixture forms a ball in the middle of the pan. (This recipe involves a lot of stirring!) Let mixture cool for five minutes; then add eggs one at a time (that's important), beating well with wooden spoon after each addition. Stir in diced cheese.

(I remember that when I made this in my thirties, my arm got really tired of beating. When I was in my sixties and working out, making it didn't bother me at all. Wow! Is there a lesson there!)

Butter an ovenproof skillet or pie pan (10 to 11 inches). Spoon puff pastry around the edges in a ring. Pour filling into the center and sprinkle it all with cheese. Bake at 400° for 40 minutes or until pastry is puffed and brown and filling is bubbling. Sprinkle with parsley and serve in wedges. (This is best served immediately, when the pastry is puffy and light. When it cools, it gets a bit soggy.)

Joel the chef.

Those were good years. We had four beautiful children. We had a charming, big, rambling, old Mediterranean-style house. We had a wide circle of friends and always had a house full of people. We also had a wild assortment of dogs—mostly show Cairn terriers and Irish wolfhounds, but we were not naturals in the show ring, and it's an expensive hobby. Eventually we also had cats, which neither of us liked, but the kids begged for them. Joel had a garden and, later, a greenhouse. He enjoyed his work as a surgeon. I had finished my Ph.D. in English and, with part-time help at home, was exploring a career as a writer. We entertained, we ate in the best restaurants in town, and we never hesitated to leave our children with babysitters. (I notice today that my children almost never leave my grandchildren with babysitters, and I'm not sure which way is best.) We weren't rich, but we weren't poor, either. We were happy.

But life goes in cycles. And so, I'm convinced, do marriages.

I hadn't worked much while I was married. Oh, sure, there were brief stints as a catalog copywriter at Tandy—a leatherworks company that is now the Tandy conglomerate—and as a pathology secretary at the local osteopathic hospital. And then there was that Ph.D. in American literature with a special interest in the literature of the American West. But we adopted our first child, Colin, while I was still finishing my dissertation. And after that, degree in hand, I became a stay-at-home mom.

I wasn't quite the kind of stay-at-home mom whom most people picture today. I'd read and taken to heart Betty Freidan's *The Feminine Mystique*, and I knew I was smart enough to need more out of life, no matter how much I loved my children. Besides, as a doctor's wife, I had that nanny who took over the house at 9 A.M., bathed, fed, and loved the children, and left at 4 P.M. That doesn't mean I didn't raise my children—I took over in the late afternoon, when the children were hungry and tired. I called it the "fussing hour," and I put

There were always lots of children around.

them to bed in the evening and woke them in the morning, and I adored them (as I still do today).

I was on my way to being a writer, though I probably didn't know it at the time, but Joel's leaving focused my attention on taking care of myself and the children. I sailed into single parenthood. Okay, it wasn't really quite that easy.

Chapter III

The Casserole Years

Joel and I were married seventeen years, fifteen of them generally very good, though with their ups and downs. We were known as a happy couple, smiled at tolerantly by his older partners for what they considered our alternative ways. We did join a country club, but we tended to wear denim when it wasn't yet accepted; we had friends who were artists, outside the circle of acceptance by the local osteopathic society. When Joel and his partners built a new office, the décor in Joel's office—bold photographs, sleek blond furniture—was in stark contrast to that of his partners. I once heard the wife of one partner explain to a visitor, "This is the office of our young partner." We had large parties, and people always filled our house— which was foreign to Joel's colleagues. In the years of the hippie movement, we were actually pretty conservative, but they didn't know that.

In the spring of 1982, Joel went to California to spend a week at a meditation center and "find himself." When he came home, he announced that he had to learn to take care of himself; he was leaving. (I later learned that he had been having an affair with the woman who has now been his wife for some twenty years. I wish her well.) But his mother was visiting—never a pleasant experience for me—and so he stayed for two weeks, acting as though everything was normal. He kissed me goodbye in the mornings and hello in the evenings. He played with the children. He worked in his garden. (When he was gone, I had to have the garden dug up and the lawn filled in with new sod—a major expense, but I could neither live with a backyard full of dying vegetable plants nor sell a house with that landscaping!) Meanwhile, I alternated between hysterical giggles and tears; I had no idea what the future held.

In truth, it's not much good analyzing what went wrong thirty-some years after the fact, and I well know that the fault, blame, credit, whatever for any divorce is shared by both parties. I think what seems charming and exciting in the passionate throes of youth pales in the responsibilities of adulthood and parenting. Joel was clearly ready to move on to another life, and I had already spent hours fantasizing about life without him—I just didn't know that was a choice I had. After all, there were those four children. They were my children, at least in my mind, and I wasn't giving them up to him. But when I fantasized about life without him, I didn't know that I could raise them alone. Of course, I found out that I could (and very well) and that his leaving was the best gift he ever gave me and the children.

The children and me in the late eighties.

In my new life, I was not only a single mom but a working woman who developed a successful career as director of a university press and as an author. But ask me how I ranked my roles in life then, and I'll give you this order: mother, author, publisher. I hope that's how my obituary reads. Now, grandmother would come second.

We lived in what I now refer to as my "doctor's wife house" for about eight months after he left. I resented that my dream house became a burden—I worried about high utility bills and necessary repairs on an older

Birthdays were always special. My mom is seated at the far end of the table on the right-hand side.

home and yard work and all the things that a man should worry about. With relief, after we sold the house, I bought a small, charming, 1920s one-story house with arched doorways, inlaid wood floors, and a wonderful, modern kitchen.

For the children's sake, I kept life so much as it had been that I was reminded of the Buddhist belief that we are but waves in the sea. When we die, the wave disappears, and the sea goes on. Joel's wave disappeared, and life went on. I kept a cheerful face; if I cried, it was in private, long after the children were asleep, and it was more from fear than from missing him. I gave tree-trimming parties, invited friends for dinner, and (most important) kept our home schedule regular. I made sure that the children ate breakfast before I saw them off to school. I welcomed them home in the afternoon— or picked them up, except that in middle school Jordan was a latchkey kid, a circumstance beyond my control. Once at a tree-trimming party (I think the first year after Joel left), someone said, "It's as if he never existed," and I smiled a little, thinking of the Buddhist saying. Another year, after I'd gone to work at TCU, a friend came and said, "I don't know anybody. But then I thought, well, of course, Judy's made a new life for herself."

I learned to be efficient. Every weekend I made a list of the nights of the week, choosing what we'd eat each night. Then I shopped for the week. I also learned to add an item to the grocery list when I used the last of it rather than trying to construct a list from memory on Saturday morning—that way I was less likely to have to rush back to the store for forgotten items. (Today, when I open a new roll of plastic wrap, for instance, I add that to my list for the week.) I tried to fix easy things, and sometimes we had leftovers, or sometimes I cooked the next night's dinner the night before. Frequently I set the dinner table before I went to work in the morning.

One January a few years ago, Jordan was thinking ahead to Thanksgiving—it would be the first all-family holiday she would host in her new home. She asked my help, and we talked about menus and who could do what and began to work out a battle plan. Then she said, "Don't tell Christian we're already talking about this—he'll think it's weird." Another time I talked to her on the Saturday before she was to entertain her in-laws on Sunday. When I asked what she was doing, she said, "Setting the table. My mother taught me that you always

Uncle Bob.

set the table a day ahead of time." And I still do for dinner parties, putting small slips of paper in dishes to indicate what food goes in which dish. At the time, Christian said to her, "You and your mother have a screw loose," but it was affectionately said.

I also adopted the French practice of the soup pot—leftovers were put into a pot each evening and kept in the refrigerator. Once a week I'd get out the pot, consider the contents, and add whatever was needed—broth, canned tomatoes, etc.—to make a palatable soup. It was usually pretty good, although it always tended to come out brown. Oh, well—in Texas, we eat a lot of brown food anyway.

Dinner was at 6:00 sharp—no excuses for not being at the table. No TV, no dinners in the family room—we gathered at the dinner table. Those dinners were important. They bound us together as a family. And we ate together until each child was working—is it coincidence that they all worked in food service?—or out of high school. Then, one by one, they drifted away to jobs, college, and girlfriends and boyfriends.

We ate a lot of casseroles.

MAKE-YOUR-OWN PIZZA

One of the earliest dishes we all made together was make-your-own pizza, back in the days when you made your own crust and didn't have Boboli or some other prepared product. I spread the dough on a rimmed jelly roll pan and covered it with pizza sauce. Then I used extra dough to section off five areas. Each child could put whatever topping wanted on his or her piece of pizza. It's a great way to cater to those who like onions and olives and those who don't.

DORIS' CASSEROLE

A friend served this years and years ago. I think it came from a Mrs. America contest winner and was simply called beef casserole, but since the hostess was Doris, we call it Doris' Casserole to this day. Doris was the wife of a radiology resident who was in training while Joel was in surgical residency—we were all poor, and our entertaining featured frugal recipes. I almost never see Doris these days, but once when I did, I told her how important her recipe was in our family, and she barely remembered the dish. I also found out that another friend at that party still serves it to her family and calls it American lasagna.

First layer:

   1 lb. ground beef

   1 14-oz. can diced tomatoes

   1 8-oz. can tomato sauce

2 cloves garlic, crushed in garlic press

2 tsp each sugar and salt (I cut back on those, but sugar is important in tomato-based sauces; my mom taught me years ago that it sort of rounds it off.)

Pepper to taste

Brown ground beef in skillet. Drain grease and return to skillet. Add tomatoes and tomato sauce, garlic, sugar, salt, and pepper. Simmer 20 minutes until it thickens a little.

Spread in a 9x13 pan.

For noodle layer:

5 oz. egg noodles (approximately—they don't come in this size pkg.)

3 oz. pkg. cream cheese

1 c. sour cream

6 green onions chopped, with some of the tops included

Topping:

1½ c. grated cheddar

Cook egg noodles and drain. While the noodles are hot, stir in cream cheese, sour cream, and green onions. Spread over meat mixture. (I gave this recipe to Bobbie, who insisted that it was backward and the noodles should go first. I finally convinced her, and her family loved it, too.) Top with grated cheddar, bake 35 minutes at 350° or until bubbly and cheese is slightly browned. Supposed to serve eight, but you'll be lucky if you can feed six with it. Freezes well.

I have a recipe for something called Hill Country casserole, which is basically the same thing, using ground venison. Haven't tried it, but I bet it would be good.

Shepherd's pie is an overlooked dish, scorned by food snobs these days. But I think its good—and the kids did, too.

SHEPHERD'S PIE

Mashed potatoes, made of about 1⅓ lbs. red potatoes. (I never skin them to mash anymore.) A good trick: put some garlic cloves in the water when you boil the potatoes. Another good one: as you add butter, salt, and pepper, substitute sour cream or cream cheese for the milk.

½ c. shredded sharp cheddar—stir into hot, freshly mashed potatoes and set aside

1 lb. lean ground beef

2 Tbsp. flour

4 c. frozen mixed vegetables (I prefer corn, green beans, and sweet peas.)

¾ c. beef broth

2 Tbsp. ketchup

¼ c. shredded sharp cheddar

Heat oven to 375°.

Brown meat in nonstick skillet (an iron skillet is always best). Stir in flour and cook briefly. Add remaining ingredients and cook, stirring, for five minutes.

Spoon into 8 in. square baking dish. Cover with mashed potatoes. Bake 20 minutes. Sprinkle remaining cheddar over the top and bake another 3-4 minutes, until cheese melts and casserole is bubbly. Serve six, but only if they're not hearty eaters.

Some people hate canned tuna. My son-in-law Brandon once sent a list to my blog of suggested uses for it: bait, fly attractant, dolphinicide, convenient source of mercury, French scent deodorant, cat food, gas mask test substance, landfill, salad ruiner, guest repellent. One dismissed him as "another food snob"—oh, could I tell her stories.

A group of friends and I once began to stage potluck "retro" dinners, serving the food we remembered from the '50s and '60s, like orange Jell-O with pineapple and shredded carrots or onion soup dip. (One naïve husband, gobbling down the dip, asked his wife if she could please get the recipe; she smiled and said, "I think I can.") One day I announced that I would fix tuna casserole for the next dinner. My recipe is pretty good, and you can adapt it to turkey or chicken. In fact, I often used it for leftover turkey after the holidays. I even cut it way down and make it for myself. A good friend later confessed that she wondered if she could really eat tuna casserole. She must have had bad memories from childhood. She thought mine was good—or said she did.

TUNA CASSEROLE

1 c. white wine

Assorted dried herbs—thyme, parsley, oregano, summer savory, tarragon, etc. (avoid Mexican spices like cumin); just throw the spices into the wine

1 small onion, chopped

½ c. celery, diced

2 Tbsp. butter

1 can cream of mushroom soup

1 7½-oz. can water-packed tuna, drained

1 c. carb filler of choice, cooked—noodles or rice

½ c. green peas

1 small can French's fried onion rings

Boil wine with herbs until the herbs turn black (about five minutes). Remove from heat.

Meanwhile sauté onion in butter. Add this to wine, along with soup. Add tuna, drained, or 1 cup diced chicken or turkey, the carb filler, and green peas for color. If there's not enough liquid for your solid ingredients, add more wine. You can also vary the amount of meat and noodles or rice to suit your taste. Put into casserole dish and top with canned fried onion rings. The size casserole dish you use will depend on how big you make your casserole, but it's best to have a shallow dish so that more of the casserole gets fried onion topping. Bake at 350° until bubbly and onions are brown.

This one only appeals to those who are adventurous enough to eat spinach, but I loved it (and still do!). It's sort of a pain to make, but I do it for special people. When Anne Isham comes to visit, I make tuna Florentine.

TUNA FLORENTINE

2 Tbsp. butter, divided use

1 small onion, minced

2 10-oz. pkgs. frozen chopped spinach

2 tsp. salt, divided use

½ tsp. ground nutmeg

2 7-oz. cans tuna, packed in oil

3 Tbsp. flour

Pinch of mace

½ tsp. white pepper

Spinach cooking liquid plus enough milk to make 1½ cups

1 c. grated Swiss cheese

2 Tbsp. Parmesan

2 Tbsp. white wine

Topping:

1½ c. soft bread crumbs

1 Tbsp. grated Parmesan

2 Tbsp. melted butter

Melt 1 Tbsp. butter; add onion and sauté until brown. Separately, cook the two packages of frozen spinach in less water than the directions call for, breaking the frozen spinach up with a wooden spoon. When tender, drain thoroughly, reserving the liquid (spinach should be very dry). Add butter and onion to spinach. Season with 1 tsp. salt and nutmeg. Simmer briefly to blend flavors.

Add milk to spinach liquid to make 1½ cups.

Drain tuna, reserving 2 Tbsp. oil; flake.

Put 2 Tbsp. tuna oil and remaining Tbsp. butter in saucepan and melt butter. Blend in flour, mace, remaining salt, and pepper. Add spinach liquid/milk mixture and stir over heat until thick and smooth. Remove from heat and add cheeses and wine. Heat until smooth again, and fold in tuna.

Layer spinach in bottom of shallow casserole. Top with tuna mixture. Mix topping ingredients together and spread over tuna layer. Bake, uncovered, at 350° until bubbly and lightly browned (35-40 minutes).

This one also has spinach, but the kids liked it. We called it gorilla casserole because the description of the recipe said you could feed twelve gorillas with it for less than $6. That was many years ago, alas, but it's still an inexpensive and filling dish.

GORILLA CASSEROLE

2½ lbs. lean ground meat

2 Tbsp. vegetable oil

2 large onions, chopped

3 ribs celery with leaves, chopped

3 large carrots, grated

2 35-oz. cans Italian-style tomatoes

1 Tbsp. salt

1½ tsp. dried oregano

1 tsp. garlic power

Pepper to taste

½ lb. pasta, (shells, egg noodles, or elbow macaroni)

2 pkgs. frozen chopped spinach, thawed and thoroughly drained

Brown ground meat in oil. Add onions, celery, and carrots and cook about 5 minutes. Stir in tomatoes, salt, oregano, garlic powder, and pepper. Bring to a boil, lower the heat, and cook covered for an hour. Separately cook pasta. Drain, rinse, and stir into meat mixture. Add spinach.

Mix thoroughly and put in two 13x9 pans, sprinkle with grated Parmesan, and bake at 350° for 30 minutes.

Serves an army.

While I'm on a spinach kick, I might as well include spinach enchiladas—another great way to use Christmas turkey.

SPINACH ENCHILADAS

1 10-oz. pkg. frozen chopped spinach

2 cans condensed cream of chicken soup

3 chopped green onions, tops included

1 4-oz. can green chilies (optional)

½ tsp. salt

1 pint sour cream

2 cups cooked and diced turkey, preferably dark meat (ah, a way to use the dark meat that nobody wants on sandwiches)

1½ c. chopped onion

4 c. grated Monterey Jack

2 dozen corn tortillas

¾ c. cooking oil

2 c. grated cheddar

Cook spinach in water with salt, drain, and mix with soup, green onions, and chilies. Puree in food processor. Add sour cream and mix. In separate mixing bowl, combine turkey, onion, and jack cheese. Dip tortillas, one at a time, in heated oil to soften. (These days many people soften them in the microwave, though I hesitate to give specific directions for that—it does cut down on grease, however.) Spread turkey mixture down center of each tortilla, roll up, and hold with a toothpick. (I sometimes skip the toothpick—what if someone ate it?) Put seam-side down in greased shallow baking dish, side by side. Pour spinach sauce over and top with cheddar. Bake at 350° for 30 minutes. Serves ten to twelve.

Another trick I've learned with enchilada casseroles lately: just layer flat tortillas and top with filling; make at least two layers of tortilla, filling, tortilla, filling, topping. Much easier than that softening in grease, and the end taste is every bit as good.

TURKEY HASH

I used to make turkey hash by dicing cooked potatoes and browning them in the skillet with some chopped onion. Add chopped turkey and enough leftover gravy to hold it all together. If you don't have leftover gravy—we never did!—use canned or even the instant packets and season with a little Worcestershire, salt, and pepper. I recently read a recipe using frozen hash browns for hash, which sounds good and easy, but I'd sure get them brown first.

There's a chicken salad casserole that I cut down and fix for myself even today. It's also great for taking to potluck suppers.

CHICKEN SALAD CASSEROLE

3 c. cooked chicken, diced

2½ c. sliced celery

2 tsp. curry powder

1 tsp. lemon juice

¾ c. mayonnaise

½ c. sour cream

2 c. crushed potato chips

1 c. shredded sharp cheddar

Mix everything but chips and cheddar and refrigerate overnight in a refrigerator-to-oven dish. Just before serving, mix crushed potato chips with grated sharp cheddar. Top casserole and run under broiler until browned and cheese is melted. Chicken salad should still be cold. Serves six. (You need a good freezer-to-oven dish to do this.)

Once I was invited—commanded?—to come to a potluck luncheon to address invitations for Women in Communication, to which I then belonged. They sent out this recipe, and it was pretty good. I've used it since.

BAKED CHICKEN SALAD CASSEROLE

    2 c. chopped chicken (about 5 breast halves)

    3 hard-boiled eggs, grated or sliced (your choice)

    2 cans cream of mushroom soup

    ½ Tbsp. lemon juice

    ¾ c. mayonnaise

    2 tsp. salt

    2 c. chopped celery

    ½ tsp. pepper

    4 tsp. onion, minced very fine

Layer chicken and eggs in a 9x13 pan. Mix everything else together and pour soup mixture over. Top with crushed potato chips. Bake at 375° for about 30 minutes or until hot.

Of course, it wasn't all casseroles. There were other dishes the kids liked. Beef and beans was Megan's particular favorite. She said recently that she hasn't had it in years and wants me to make it.

BEEF AND BEANS

    2 c. dried red kidney beans

    1 Tbsp. oil

    1 c. chopped onion

    1 lb. ground beef

    4 Tbsp. beef-base granules (or equivalent in bouillon cubes)

    1 Tbsp. sugar

    1 tsp. black pepper

    1 tsp. garlic powder

    Hot cooked rice

Soak beans overnight in cold water to cover. Drain, cover with fresh water, and bring to a boil. Lower heat and simmer one hour. Do not drain. (Canned beans won't work—you need the broth that comes from cooking them yourself.)

Heat oil and brown onion and ground beef. Add to cooked beans and liquid. Stir in seasonings and simmer until you're sure all is heated and beans are tender.

Serve over hot cooked rice. Don't cheat on the bouillon or sugar—both are essential.

One year on our annual ski trip to Santa Fe, Tina and Andy Miracle invited us for supper—it's true friends who would take on my whole crew. I think Andy did most of the cooking for this, and later they were kind enough to share the recipe.

SOUTHWESTERN CHICKEN SOUP
   1 Tbsp. olive oil
   1 c. chopped onion
   ½ c. chopped celery
   6 c. chicken stock
   4 chicken breasts
   4 chicken thighs
   ½ c. uncooked rice
   1 10-oz. pkg. frozen corn
   1 tsp. cumin
   1 Tbsp. chili powder
   2 Tbsp. picante sauce
   1 14-oz. can diced tomatoes
   1 4-oz. can chopped chilies
   Grated Monterey Jack and cheddar cheese
   In soup kettle, sauté celery and onion in olive oil until soft. Add chicken stock, chicken pieces, and uncooked rice. Bring to boil. Reduce heat and simmer about half an hour.

Remove chicken and set aside. Simmer liquids another 15 minutes. (You don't want to simmer the chicken so long that it gets tough.) Take the chicken off the bones and return to the stock, with the remaining ingredients. Heat through and taste for seasoning. Add cheese at serving.

I once was in the process of making chicken with herbs when Uncle Bob called and wanted me to go see the children ride their horses. Of course, I put the chicken in the oven, turned the heat low and left it. It was delicious when we finally got back. Ordinary directions call for baking it at 450° for 10 minutes and then reducing heat to 350° for 30 to 40 minutes.

CHICKEN WITH HERBS

8 joined chicken legs and thighs (I usually just use thighs –for economy and because the thigh and leg are too much for many of us to eat.)
½ stick butter
Juice of 1 lemon
½ c. mixed finely chopped fresh herbs—thyme, tarragon, rosemary, whatever you want but probably not the Mexican spices
2 tsp. salt
¾ cup dry white wine
Melt the butter in an oven-to-table pan and add lemon juice. Turn chicken in butter mixture to coat thoroughly. Place in pan skin side up. Mix chopped herbs with salt and sprinkle over the chicken. If baking the traditional way, add the wine when you cut the oven temperature back to 350°.
At serving, spoon pan juices over the chicken.

We seem to have eaten a lot of chicken, but we couldn't afford steak— and I didn't get a lot of complaints. The kids particularly liked stir-fry, which I sort of made up as I went along, trying to include the vegetables that most of the kids would eat: broccoli, onions, green beans, sprouts, pea pods, sliced water chestnuts, cauliflower, and celery.

CHICKEN STIR-FRY

½ c. chicken broth
3 Tbsp. soy sauce
1 Tbsp. cornstarch
2 Tbsp. cooking oil, preferably vegetable

1 tsp. grated fresh ginger root

1 minced or pressed garlic clove

Diced raw chicken, white meat only, about ½ breast per person

Vegetables of choice – probably count on ¾ cup vegetables per person

If using broccoli, cauliflower, or celery, blanch until crisp-tender.

Mix chicken broth, soy sauce, and cornstarch and set aside.

Heat cooking oil in wok (or a good heavy skillet). Stir-fry ginger root and garlic.

Add chicken. Cook until almost done. Add vegetables and cook, stirring constantly. Stir chicken broth mixture into vegetables and meat. Cook until bubbly.

Serve with cooked rice or Chinese noodles, and pass the soy sauce.

This marinade was meant for shish kebobs, but it's great for grilled chicken.

TERIYAKI CHICKEN

2 lbs. chicken, either whole breasts or cut in strips

1 garlic clove, minced

2 Tbsp. minced onion

2 Tbsp. oil

¼ c. soy sauce or to taste

3 Tbsp. sherry (I use whatever white wine I have on hand, which is usually chardonnay—drier than sherry but less full-bodied.)

1 Tbsp. lemon juice

1 Tbsp. sugar

1 tsp. salt

2 tsp. ginger

½ tsp. pepper

Mix all ingredients except the chicken and stir thoroughly. Marinate chicken and grill or sauté lightly. You can thread it on to shish kebob skewers with fresh vegetables and brush the vegetables with the marinade. As long as the marinade gets cooked, it's safe and okay.

We did grill some in the casserole years, mostly hamburgers, but green chili chicken breasts were a favorite recipe. You have to start this one the night before. Serves eight.

GREEN CHILI CHICKEN BREASTS

⅔ c. fresh lemon juice, divided (since the recipe also calls for grated lemon peel, do that before you juice the lemons)

¼ c. minced parsley

1 4-oz. can chopped chilies

2 Tbsp. fresh rosemary

2 Tbsp. fresh thyme, minced (I find fresh almost too strong and usually use 1 tsp. of dried thyme, even though I have thyme in my herb garden.)

2 Tbsp. minced garlic

4 tsp. salt, divided

6 bone-in chicken breasts

⅔ c. dry white wine

½ tsp. grated lemon peel

2 tsp. coarse ground pepper

Mix ⅓ c. lemon juice, parsley, chilies, rosemary, thyme, garlic, and 2 tsp. salt.

Carefully loosen the chicken skin so that you can spread the herb mixture between the skin and the meat. Arrange chicken in baking pan in single layer. Splash white wine over it, with remaining ⅓ c. lemon juice, lemon peel, pepper, and remaining salt. Turn chicken to coat. Chill overnight.

About an hour or a little more before serving, remove chicken from marinade but save the marinade. Put chicken skin side up, over medium heat in a covered grill and cook 15 minutes, turning occasionally. Cover and cook until skin on chicken pieces is crisp, meat is tender, and juices run clear. Baste occasionally with reserved marinade. Should cook at least 30 minutes, probably longer. (My kids absolutely hated being served chicken that was the least bit pink—and rightly so.)

This is a favorite recipe that I still cook today. When I first started fixing it for my family, chicken fingers were not as popular as they are today, and you had to cut your own. I think we called this chicken strips. Same thing, still good.

CHICKEN FINGERS WITH GARLIC BUTTER
  2 whole boneless chicken breasts, cut into fingers (about 2 lbs.)
  Salt and pepper to taste
  1 Tbsp. fresh oregano or 2 tsp. dried
  2 Tbsp. flour
  2 Tbsp. butter
  2 Tbsp. oil
  4 plum tomatoes, skinned, seeded and diced
  1 Tbsp. chopped garlic
  4 Tbsp. fresh basil, minced
  2 Tbsp. lime juice
  Mix salt, pepper, oregano, and flour in flat dish. Coat chicken pieces. Heat butter and oil in skillet. Sauté chicken pieces in a single layer until browned. Add tomatoes and garlic and cook about a few minutes. Add basil and lime juice, and serve to six people. (In this one, the lime juice makes the difference. I have cheated and substituted drained, diced, canned tomatoes.)

When I fixed pot roast (a fairly straightforward recipe, I thought), Uncle Bob said: "You always cook with unusual seasonings, don't you?" I didn't think this was all that unusual, but it sure makes good gravy.

POT ROAST
  1 3-4-lb. pot roast, shoulder or rump
  Flour, salt, and pepper
  Butter
  1 can mushroom soup
  1 envelope dry onion soup mix

1/2 c. red wine

Potatoes

Carrots

Dredge roast in flour, salt and pepper, and brown on all sides in butter. Separately mix soup, onion soup mix, and red wine. Pour over roast and cook at 325° for three hours in oven, or all day in a crockpot or a sturdy pot in a low oven.

Somewhere along the way, add cut potatoes and chunks of carrots. Cook long enough that they become tender. Should serve six.

Melanie recently told me about this wonderful short-ribs recipe that a friend had given her. It was the same recipe, minus the wine. I said, "I've been doing that for years, only I add something else." She laughed and said, "I know you—it's wine!"

Aunt Amy is a beloved New York aunt and a good cook.

AUNT AMY'S GIANT STUFFED HAMBURGER

2 Tbsp. butter

1¼ c. herbed, seasoned stuffing mix, crushed (makes about ¾ cup)

1 egg, beaten

1 3-oz. can mushrooms, drained (You could use sautéed fresh, which would be good; I omit them these days because Christian, Brandon, Jamie and Melanie think mushrooms are poison.)

⅓ c. beef broth

¼ c. sliced green onion

¼ c. toasted almonds

¼ c. snipped parsley (optional, but a nice touch)

1 tsp. lemon juice

2 lbs. ground beef

1 tsp. salt

Melt butter in saucepan and remove from heat. Add stuffing mix, egg, mushrooms, beef broth, onion, almonds, parsley, and lemon juice. (It's

remarkable what adding lemon or lime juice does to a variety of recipes!) Mix well and set aside.

Combine beef and salt and divide in half. On sheets of waxed paper (I
have one of the few old-fashioned kitchens where there is still a roll of
waxed paper), pat each half into an 8-inch circle. Spoon stuffing over
one circle of meat to within 1 inch of edge. Top with second circle of
meat and peel off waxed paper. Seal around edges and invert into a
well-greased grilling basket. Grill over medium heat about 10-12 minutes per side. Cut into wedges and serve. Makes six servings.

Don't have a grill or it's too cold outside? Broil it in the oven—it still
tastes great. Just don't overcook it and get it dry.

The first time I ever made stuffed cabbage was in Missouri, before Joel
and I married. I was going to feed him and some of his single Jewish friends
from back east. I got a recipe (from *The Joy of Cooking)* and followed it
carefully, including topping the dish with gingersnaps. It was a lot of work!
Each of those boys walked by the stove, lifted the pot lid, and said, "Mom
never did it like that!" For many years, stuffed cabbage was a rarity at our
house because it was such a pain to boil the cabbage, peel the leaves and
stuff them. Then I found this recipe.

STUFFED CABBAGE
1 head green cabbage
1 lb. ground beef
1 onion, diced
1 garlic clove, minced
1 tsp. salt
½ tsp. pepper
1 c. cooked rice
2½ c. water

Tomato sauce:

    28-oz. can tomatoes with liquid

    6 oz. can tomato paste

    1 Tbsp. brown sugar

    ½ tsp. salt

    ½ tsp. Worcestershire sauce

    ⅛ tsp. ground allspice

Make tomato sauce by boiling all ingredients, reducing heat, and simmering 20 minutes. Put aside.

Discard tough outer leaves of cabbage and remove two large leaves—set aside. Cut out stem and center of cabbage, leaving a shell of about 1 inch. Discard the stem and chop remaining cabbage.

In Dutch oven or skillet, cook beef, onion, garlic, salt, pepper, and 1 cup diced cabbage until meat is brown and cabbage is tender—maybe 20 minutes. Add rice and 1 cup of the tomato sauce.

Fill the cabbage center with the meat mixture. Use the saved cabbage leaves to cover the opening. Tie pieces of string around the cabbage to hold the added leaves in place. Set aside.

Add water to Dutch oven and scrape to loosen brown bits. Add remaining diced cabbage and tomato sauce. Put the stuffed cabbage, stem-end down, in the sauce, heat to boiling and then simmer about 90 minutes. When you walk by the stove and think about it, baste the cabbage.

Put the cabbage on a platter, cut side down, cut the strings, and spoon the sauce over it. Cut into wedges. Serves six.

STUFFED CABBAGE THE REAL WAY

I do have an excellent recipe for stuffed cabbage, sans gingersnaps, that I got from an older doctor's wife.

    Garlic cloves

    1 small head cabbage

    1 lb. cooked ground lamb

1 14-oz. can diced tomatoes, drained

Instant rice (I have no idea how much)

Salt and pepper

Pinch of cinnamon (optional)

Tomato juice

Soften cabbage leaves in hot water after carefully peeling them from the head.

Mix ground lamb, tomatoes, rice, salt, and pepper. Put a spoonful of meat mixture in a cabbage leaf, fold ends over, and shape into a roll—you may have to use toothpicks to keep it together. (Like old-fashioned cooks, she gave me no quantities—I just scribbled this on a piece of scrap paper as she talked.) If it's any help, you can probably count on most diners eating two rolls, if you serve mashed potatoes with them.

Scatter garlic cloves generously over the bottom of your baking dish. Cover with those cabbage leaves you didn't use. Then add the rolls on top of the cabbage. Dot with butter and pour tomato juice over all. Bake (you're sort of on your own here). But I've made it often, and it's really good—just a lot of work.

I did occasionally cook pork. This one was a quick and easy favorite.

MUSTARD PORK

1¼ lb. pork tenderloin

Dijon mustard

2 Tbsp. butter

½ c. beef broth

½ tsp. dried tarragon

½ c. half-and-half

Slice the tenderloin into pieces about 1½ inches thick. Flatten slightly with meat mallet. Cover one side of each slice with Dijon mustard. Melt butter in skillet, add pork, mustard side down, and cook 5 minutes on each side. Make sure there's no pink in the center. Transfer meat to ovenproof dish and put in low oven to keep warm. Add beef broth and tarragon to pan drippings. Stir to scrape up brown bits. Simmer until half the liquid evaporates. Add half-and-half and simmer until slightly thickened. To serve, pour sauce over pork slices. Serves two generously, usually three. Good served with egg noodles or mashed potatoes.

This is an easy and very good version of a sometimes complicated dish. My kids didn't like it because they didn't like eggplant, but I remember that my brother liked it. And I still like it and may cook it again soon.

EGGPLANT PARMESAN

2 eggplants

2 lbs. ground beef

2 cloves garlic, crushed

2 16-oz. cans diced tomatoes

2 6-oz. cans tomato paste

1 tsp. salt

Pepper to taste

Pinch of sugar

3 c. bread crumbs (about 6 slices)

⅔ c. grated Parmesan

Vegetable oil, as needed; start with 3 Tbsp. but eggplant really soaks up oil and you may need to add more as you go along

Halve two eggplants lengthwise and hollow out, leaving shells about ¼ inch thick. Cube eggplant that you've cut out and sauté in vegetable oil until soft. Drain well on paper towels. Brown beef; add garlic, tomatoes, tomato paste, salt, pepper, and sugar and simmer 15 minutes. Stir in bread crumbs, sautéed eggplant, and Parmesan.

Spoon into eggplant shells. It won't all fit, so use an extra side dish. Top with sliced mozzarella and bake. Will probably feed five, but only four get the eggplant halves. The fifth person has to eat out of a small oven dish.

A real estate agent named Carolyn Burk took me under her wing when Joel was still in a residency and never abandoned me. After the divorce, she was one of my strongest cheerleaders, and my appreciation for her is beyond bounds. Joel and I rented our second house in Fort Worth from her, after asking her to show us a house that we could no more afford than we could afford a mansion in the city's most exclusive districts. But she must have sensed that I needed help—and later I was in a position to help her youngest son. Somewhere along the way, she gave me a chicken loaf recipe. To me, this is the best pure chicken flavor I've ever had.

CHICKEN LOAF

1 chicken hen or 2 fryers
1 cylinder saltine crackers
2 envelopes unflavored gelatin

Stew chicken until cooked thoroughly. Reserve the stock. Cool chicken and pull meat off bones. Chop finely. (Carolyn did it with scissors, but I use the food processor, being careful not to over-process.) Grind one cylinder of saltines in food processor and add to chicken.

Soften gelatin in ½ c. of reserved stock. Add to chicken along with enough stock to bind it together—it should be moist but not soupy. (Sometimes I use a bouillon cube to give the stock more flavor. I know Carolyn never added gelatin, but for me it holds the loaf together—my kids say it makes the loaf "gelatinous" And they don't mean that in a good way.)

Pack into a loaf pan. Cover with clear wrap, put another loaf pan on top, and weigh it down with canned goods. Refrigerate overnight.

Good with mayonnaise. This will freeze but will not keep after defrosting.

One dish that everyone at my house loved was salmon croquettes. For a while the high school daughter of friends was living with us—they had moved, and Jeanine wanted to finish her senior year at her school. A single pediatrician who was a good friend frequently showed up for dinner. One night, Jeanine exploded as she saw his car turn into the driveway: "Why does he always show up when we're having salmon croquettes?"

I always made at least a double batch. My mom taught me to disregard those recipes that call for mashed potatoes—always use ground saltines. I still frequently use a 7½-oz. can of salmon and make these for myself. They make great sandwiches the next day, with mayonnaise.

SALMON CROQUETTES
1 14.75-oz. can of pink salmon (Pick the bones out if you can, and discard the black skin.)
One small onion, chopped
Dash of Worcestershire
Salt and pepper to taste
Pinch of dry mustard
2 eggs
Ground saltine crackers
Beat everything but the crackers together and then add enough ground crackers to make it a mixture you can shape with your hands into logs about three inches long. Roll each log in more ground crackers, and sauté until browned on all sides (doesn't take long). Serve with lemon or ketchup. Most diners will eat two croquettes.

A friend gave me a recipe for wine casserole, which turned out so much like sloppy Joe that I called it that when I served it. Recently Megan asked for the recipe and cooked it for Brandon, who pronounced that it was really good but it wasn't sloppy Joe, which to him was meat and ketchup. (I think that's a simplistic description.) But Meg e-mailed me caustically that she guessed she was the only one who grew up thinking red wine was an essential ingredient of sloppy Joe. You can serve this on toasted buns or just in a bowl, like a stew.

JUDY'S SLOPPY JOE
1 lb. ground beef
1 15-oz. can of beans (any kind you want), rinsed and drained
½ c. chopped onion

½ c. diced celery

2 Tbsp. bacon drippings (If you can't bring yourself to use it in this health-conscious age, use vegetable oil, but the bacon flavor really makes a difference.)

1½ c. canned tomatoes

¼ c. ketchup

1½ Tbsp. Worcestershire

Dash of Tabasco

1 tsp. salt

⅛ tsp. pepper

¼ tsp. oregano

¼ c. dry red wine

1 Tbsp. A-1 sauce (If I don't have this, omit it; I can never tell the difference.)

Cook onion in bacon drippings. Add beef and brown. Add remaining ingredients and simmer 20 to 30 minutes.

Chili is, of course, a Texas favorite, and everyone has an exotic recipe. I'm not fond of really hot peppers, and the chili I serve is simple and hearty, if not exactly a gourmet choice. Neither is it very spicy. Beans are controversial in Texas—purists say they have no place in chili. But I drain, rinse, and add Ranch Style canned beans. I think this is great made with venison.

JUDY'S MILD AND TENTATIVE CHILI

1 lb. ground beef or chili cut venison

Enough oil to sauté onion, garlic and beef

1 large onion, chopped

1 clove garlic, chopped

1 8-oz. can tomato sauce

1 cup beer

4 tsp. chili powder or to taste

½ tsp. Tabasco

2 tsp. salt

2 c. beans

Brown onion and garlic; add hamburger and cook until all pink is gone.

Add everything else except beans and simmer for 60 to 90 minutes. Stir occasionally, and add more beer as needed (you've got that open warm beer anyway). Taste and add more chili powder as needed. Add beans and heat just before serving.

My family likes to top it with chopped purple onion and grated cheddar.

Vegetable dishes are hard with growing children. If they're going to have dislikes, that's where they'll be. Jamie used to eat almost anything I served him, from spinach to beets (which he now tells me he doesn't like), so whenever he announced that he didn't like something, I respected it. My sons-in-law, on the other hand, hardly touch any vegetables, and Jordan won't eat asparagus or spinach, which I think are the most wonderful green things ever discovered.

My niece tasted this potato dish not too long ago and said, "I remember you used to make that." I still love it, and so do Jordan and Christian. In the cookbook in which I found the original recipe, it's called Polka Dot Salad and called for cut-up hot dogs. I've doctored the recipe, leaving out the sugar, adding the celery, and omitting the hot dogs.

GERMAN POTATO SALAD

3-4 slices bacon, fried and crumbled; reserve grease

3 stalks celery, chopped

4 green onions

1 heaping Tbsp. flour

½ c. each water and vinegar

1 Tbsp. prepared mustard

2 cans sliced white potatoes (The original recipe called for fresh cooked potatoes, of course, but this is one of the few places where I think canned does just fine and is actually better—they don't crumble like fresh-cooked potatoes.)

After you fry the bacon, if there's too much grease in the skillet, drain some, but you want a bit to cook this. Sauté celery and green onions in bacon grease. Add flour and stir.

Add water and vinegar—more of each as needed until sauce is a good consistency. Add mustard. Add potatoes. Crumble bacon and stir in. Sprinkle with parsley just before serving to add color.

A side dish I wish I'd known about in the casserole years was given me by a high school friend recently; to my joy, Barbara Bucknell Ashcraft and I have picked up our friendship again through e-mail correspondence. This was from her stepmom, and it couldn't be easier.

LOUELLA'S RICE

1 c. Minute Rice

1 c. sour cream

1 c. shredded sharp cheddar

1 can cream of celery soup

1 4-oz. can chopped chilies

Mix and bake at 350° for 35-40 minutes.

I used to make a jellied gazpacho; it sounds old-fashioned in this day when tomato aspic is passé, but this is good. And it doesn't use tomato juice for the jelled part. Once I came home from work, anticipating savoring the one tiny piece of gazpacho left in the refrigerator. Uncle Bob was lying on the couch, and the gazpacho was gone. "A man came in and pointed a gun at my head and said, 'Eat it,'" he explained.

JELLIED GAZPACHO

2 envelopes unflavored gelatin

1½ c. beef broth

¼ c. wine vinegar

2 tsp. Worcestershire

2 Tbsp. lemon juice

1 tsp. salt

⅛ tsp. Tabasco

3 c. chopped tomatoes

½ c. chopped celery

¼ c. chopped onion

1 clove garlic, minced

Mix gelatin with cold broth and let it stand a bit while you chop vegetables. Then heat it until the gelatin is dissolved. Remove from heat and stir in next five ingredients. Chill until salad is about as thick as egg whites. Stir in remaining ingredients. I used to do it in a 6-cup ring mold and set a small bowl of mayonnaise in the middle. Serves six to eight.

"Life is uncertain, so eat dessert first," advises an old saying. We were not much on desserts, but the children made cookies at a young age, seriously bent over the kitchen table, dropping chocolate chip cookie dough in spoonfuls on the cookie sheet or pressing peanut butter cookies with a fork to get the crisscross lines. Throughout their growing-up years they made cookies and brownies (often from a mix). But we also had a few "made-from-scratch" recipes, such as the chocolate chip and peanut butter cookies from my childhood (see first chapter for recipes).

Here's what I cooked when we did have dessert:

My grandmother's banana cake recipe makes wonderful cupcakes. Over the years, I made an amazing number of cupcakes and used lots of more expensive ingredients just to avoid throwing out two overripe bananas. In retrospect, it was foolish penny-pinching, but the children usually ate the cupcakes, and today the girls have asked for the recipe.

BANANA DROP CAKES

1½ c. sugar

½ c. butter or margarine, softened

2 eggs

2 large or 3 small bananas, very ripe, mashed

1 tsp. baking soda mixed with 4 Tbsp. sour milk (sour by adding a bit of vinegar)

2 c. flour (more if needed, but do not make it too stiff)

Cream butter and sugar. Add eggs. Add bananas. Alternately add flour and sour milk mixture. Bake in muffin pans (I *always* use muffin cups) at 350° for 20 to 25 minutes. (Mom used to ice them, but I think that's gilding the lily.)

Megan loves lemon desserts, and a friend who knows that gave me this recipe.

WHIPPERSNAPPERS

1 lemon cake mix

1 egg

2 c. Cool Whip

Mix until smooth; drop by heaping tablespoons in powdered sugar and roll to coat; bake on greased cookie sheet at 350° for 10 to 12 minutes. Should be slightly tan but not hard. (You can also do this with chocolate, spice, or yellow cake mix.)

A favorite aunt of mine used to make these cookies, and I remember that Colin particularly liked them.

SNICKERDOODLES

1 c. margarine

1 c. Crisco (I bet today you could use margarine)

3 c. sugar

4 eggs

5½ c. flour

4 tsp. cream of tartar

2 tsp. soda

½ tsp. salt

4 Tbsp. sugar

4 tsp. cinnamon

Cream margarine, Crisco, sugar, and eggs. Combine dry ingredients, except sugar and cinnamon, and mix into soft cookie dough. Chill. Seperately mix together cinnamon and sugar. Shape dough into 1- to 1½-inch balls and roll in cinnamon/sugar mixture. Place 3 inches apart on ungreased cookie sheet. Bake at 400° for 8 to 10 minutes.

A good friend gave me this dessert recipe and advised walking five miles after eating.

TEXAS DELIGHT

First layer:

1 stick melted margarine

1 c. flour

1 tsp. salt

½ c. crushed pecans

Press in pan and bake for 10 minutes at 325-350°.

Second layer:

8 oz. cream cheese

1 c. Cool Whip

½ c. granulated sugar

Spread over first layer.

Third layer:

2 pkg. pudding made from Jell-O instant mix (chocolate or whatever flavor you want—is there any other flavor but chocolate?)

Top with Cool Whip and chopped nuts.

This bundt cake is great for crowds. Colin was in nursery school with a girl named Mary Helen. Once there was to be a potluck dinner at a parents' meeting, but instead of letting parents bring whatever they wanted, there was one recipe for the main dish, salad, dessert, etc. If you signed up to make the main dish, for instance, you made turkey tetrazzini. I elected to bring the dessert, which was Mary Helen's Mother's Coffee Cake. I had never made a bundt cake before, and when I let the cake cool and tried to take it out of the pan, half came out and half stayed behind. I called a friend, who explained that you had to let it sit *only* five minutes and then turn it out. So I made another cake, and thereafter Mary Helen's father called me the "two-cake lady."

You can make this any flavor you want. I always do chocolate, but you can mix banana cake and banana pudding. Or vanilla or lemon. A friend of mine recently tried strawberry and liked it, though I retain some doubts about that.

MARY HELEN'S MOTHER'S COFFEE CAKE

1 box cake mix
1 box instant pudding
½ c. oil
4 eggs
1½ c. sour cream
Sugar and cinnamon
Mix together everything but sugar and cinnamon. Spray bundt pan with Pam or similar coating. Mix cinnamon and sugar and sprinkle on all sides of prepared pan. Add the batter, evening it out as much as possible (it's a thick batter), and top with cinnamon and sugar. Bake at 350° for 50 to 60 minutes (check with a long kebab skewer or something similar); it often has to cook longer. Cool five minutes and remove from the pan. *Don't wait any longer.* Run a knife around edges of pan and tunnel in the middle, and then top with a plate, invert, and gently shake to remove the cake from the pan.

The nice thing about this, if you care, is that you can make it fairly healthy if you use egg substitutes and low-fat sour cream. I always had to hide the cartons from Colin if I did that because he objects loudly to low-fat products, but it works.

Recently I made a bundt cake that called for 2½ sticks of butter and 5 eggs. It wasn't nearly as good as my regular bundt cake—and a lot more work.

But truly, we didn't have time for dessert. I had gone to work at TCU. A friend was leaving the position of coordinator of community services, and I took over the job, working three-quarter time so I could be home with the children after school. They attended an elementary school across the street from the campus and then were bused to middle school.

Bobbie and me at a "pound cake party".

I remember one day when I walked over to the school to meet Jamie. I can see him yet, barreling down the sidewalk, a huge grin on his face, and arms spread for a hug. I immediately got down on one knee, and he came so fast and hugged so tightly that I nearly fell over. It's one of those frozen-in-time memories that is planted in my heart forever.

While working at TCU, I was also starting my writing career. My first novel, *After Pa Was Shot,* was published as a juvenile novel by the now-gone William Morrow and Company. Instantly, I was categorized as a juvenile novelist—a categorization that has stuck over the years—so I set about writing more young adult novels. After a wildly unsuccessful second try, TCU Press published *Luke and the Van Zandt County War,* which won the Best Juvenile Fiction Award from the Texas Institute of Letters in 1984. Uncle Bob and the children trooped to San Antonio with me to receive the award. The woman who presented it was distinctly untactful, saying that so-and-so who usually won hadn't entered that year, and so the award was going to me.

Still, I dreamt of a career, fame, and fortune, rivaling perhaps Judy Blume. That never happened, and I learned some hard but true lessons about publishing. But I was busy, and the kids and I were happy.

My dad died in 1977. He and Mom were living in North Carolina at the time, but Mom sold the house and moved to Fort Worth shortly thereafter. And she began having Sunday dinners again—those memories from our childhood. At the time, my brother John and I were both still happily married (or thought we were happy), and Mom's six grandchildren were all small. Her table held eight, which meant that only two grandchildren ate at the table. The other four ate at the "children's table." Mom put a card table near an antique trunk in the dining room and put three chairs around it. One child got to sit on the trunk—a privilege over which they fought noisily. We would hear cries of "You sat on the trunk last week!" and "It's my turn to sit at the big people's table."

Sunday dinners continued after both John and I divorced, but there came the day when Mom could no longer do them. Cooking for the family became my responsibility, although Mom continued to join us. Certainly Sunday nights in my household—noisy, crowded, full of laughter—were a far cry from the quiet Sunday

Uncle Charles and Aunt Reva on their 50th anniversary .

night suppers before the fireplace that I remembered from childhood. But I remembered that Sunday night was a special time, a family time, and I wanted my children to have that sense. The difference was that we had a large extended family.

An assortment of people joined us—friends and relatives. We always held hands and said the grace that the children had learned in preschool. Uncle John would say, "Start 'em out, Jamie," and all heads bowed as Jamie said the first word, "God" and then we all joined in,

". . . is great, God is good;
Let us thank him for this food.
By his hand we are fed;
Give us, Lord, our daily bread."

In the jeep at Arc Ridge Ranch, with Mom and Uncle Charles in the front.

These days when we celebrate holidays with John's family—now also large—we still say that, though recently Madison was the one to start it. I confess to tears of sentiment and joy.

Next, Uncle John would go around the table, asking each of us to tell something that happened during the week. The children—my four and his two, Jennifer and Russell—groaned and rolled their eyes, but they always came up with something.

And then there was the infamous Thanksgiving dinner when he asked everyone to tell what he or she was thankful for. It was uneventful until the turn came to a young man Megan had dated just once or twice but who had joined us. Robbie stood and very seriously said, "I'm grateful for Megan and her beauty." Megan blushed furiously, and her siblings and cousins had to cover their mouths to keep from hooting. The rest of us were stunned speechless.

The moment passed but was never forgotten. To this day, someone will say, "I'm grateful for Megan and her beauty," and everyone dissolves in laughter, with Meg laughing as heartily as anyone.

The conversation ranged over many areas at these dinner tables. We tried to avoid politics; John and I are emphatically on opposite sides of the fence, and neither of us handles that well. Sometimes we talked about the osteopathic college, where both John and Mary Lu taught and where I had once worked, and sometimes about TCU since there were years when many of us were involved in the university in one way or another—Colin, Megan, and Jamie all attended TCU. I think we did really try not to let the conversation deteriorate into silliness or meaningless jabber.

Nowadays if I think about feeding twelve to sixteen people on a regular basis, I'm sort of overwhelmed. But I did it every week. And I can't really remember all the things I cooked—soups, stews, chili, and double or triple recipes of casseroles. Budget was a consideration for me, though John usually brought the wine.

I remember when one night I served a hamburger/black-eyed pea/cornbread mix. TCU Press at the time was publishing a book titled *Eats: A Folk History of Texas Food,* and I thought it would be interesting to try out some of the recipes. In fact, I think the late Jerry Flemmons, *Fort Worth Star-Telegram* travel editor, recommended this one to me, saying his ex-wife was from Athens (Texas), the black-eyed-pea capital of the world, and used to fix it. John took one bite, looked at me, and asked: "Sis, is the budget the problem?" I stopped experimenting with historical recipes.

I didn't usually get too fancy. Soups and stews were easy.

CHICKEN AND CORN STEW

    2 lbs. chicken pieces
    4 c. water
    4 medium potatoes, diced
    1 large onion, chopped
    1 15-oz. can tomato sauce
    1 can peeled, diced tomatoes
    Salt and pepper
    1 tsp. chili powder
    1 tsp. paprika
    1 16-oz. can whole kernel corn
    1 16 oz. can cream-style corn

Cook chicken in lightly salted water until tender. Remove chicken, cool, debone, and dice. Save the cooking liquid. Add potatoes and onion and cook until tender. If necessary, add more water.

Add everything but the corn and bring to a boil. Add the two corns and reduce the heat. Simmer for 15 minutes in covered pot. Serves eight but is easily doubled.

I asked Mary Lu, a frequent Sunday night guest, what I used to cook, and she answered, "King Ranch chicken." That's such a standard that I assume everyone knows about it, so including it here is a little obvious. But I do remember serving it one time to Bill Sheridan, who had never had it and thought it was the best thing ever.

KING RANCH CHICKEN

2 whole chicken breasts, boneless
16 corn tortillas, torn into small pieces
2 medium onions, chopped
1 can cream of mushroom soup
1 can cream of chicken soup
½-1 can Rotel tomatoes
Grated cheddar

I used to tell people, "Well, you start by boiling an old hen." But now I roast chicken breasts—so much easier. Season with salt, pepper, and a few slices of onion. Put in pan and cover with foil. Roast at 350° for 30 to 40 minutes. Cool and chop finely. Layer, in a greased casserole: tortillas, chicken, onion; repeat layers. Pour over all a mixture of soups and tomatoes (how much tomato you use depends on how hot you want it to be). Cover with grated cheese and bake at 350° until cheese melts and is brown and casserole is bubbly.

I had a sort of standard Tex-Mex casserole that varied the formula by adding cottage cheese and olives (which I omitted because I don't like them). This is supposed to serve twelve, but we usually had half of it left over to eat during the week after Sunday night supper. I recently fixed it for a friend when there was a death in the family, and she said her family liked it so much that they would pay outrageous amounts of money for the recipe. I told her they could buy the book.

TEX-MEX CASSEROLE

    4 lbs. ground round or chuck

    2 large onions, chopped

    2 minced garlic cloves

    ¼ cup chili powder, or more to taste

    6 c. tomato sauce

    1 tsp. sugar

    1½ tsp. salt

    2 4-oz cans chopped green chilies

    Brown meat in skillet. Add onions, garlic, and chili powder. While meat cooks, soften 24 corn tortillas in small frying pan or microwave. Separately, mix

    4 cups small-curd cottage cheese

    2 eggs

    Have ready:

    1 lb. thinly sliced Jack cheese

    2 cups grated cheddar

    Grease a six-quart casserole (I use my big paella pan). Layer meat sauce, half the Jack cheese, half the cottage cheese/egg mixture, and half the softened tortillas. Repeat, finishing with a final layer of meat. Cover with grated cheddar and bake, uncovered, at 350° for 30 minutes. Pass chopped green onions and sour cream.

A Tex-Mex dish I've discovered more recently and think might be my favorite ever:

TAMALE PIE WITH POLENTA

   1 lb. ground sirloin, as fat-free as possible (now I use buffalo)

   1½ Tbsp. chili powder

   1 Tbsp. ground cumin

   1 16-oz. bottle medium hot salsa (Pace picante preferred)

   1 15-oz. can refried beans (original flavor)

   1¾ c. chicken broth (preferably from organic carton rather than canned)

   ½ c. chopped cilantro

   2 1-lb. rolls prepared polenta, sliced ¼ inch thick

   3½ c. shredded sharp cheddar

Brown beef, breaking up clumps. Add chili powder and cumin. Stir briefly. Add salsa, beans, and broth. Simmer until thick, about 10 minutes. Add the cilantro. Salt and pepper to taste.

Layer half the polenta in a greased 9x13 baking dish. Top with sauce and 1½ c. cheese. Top with remaining polenta and then remaining cheddar. Bake uncovered at 350° for 35 minutes. Let it sit a minute before serving.

One night to celebrate my mom's birthday, I fixed an elegant crab-and-artichoke casserole—she loved crab. This serves at least ten people.

CRAB AND ARTICHOKE CASSEROLE

   1 stick butter

   3 Tbsp. minced onion

   ½ c. flour

   4 c. half-and-half

   ½ c. sherry

   Salt and pepper

   Juice of one lemon

   4 c. fresh or canned crab meat

   2 cans artichoke hearts, drained (I much prefer canned over frozen)

   2½ c. cooked pasta (not thin spaghetti—maybe small shells or egg noodles)

   2 c. grated Gruyére cheese

Melt butter in a heavy skillet; add onion and sauté until light brown.

Add flour and stir until flour begins to brown a bit (do NOT burn). Remove from heat.

Separately heat half-and-half to near boiling and add to onion and flour mixture, beating hard to keep it from lumping.

Return to stove, medium heat, and stir until it boils. Turn the heat down and add sherry. Season with salt and pepper.

Meanwhile, cook pasta until just al dente. Drain and rinse with cold water.

Separately pour lemon juice over the crab and toss. Combine with drained artichoke hearts. Add pasta and sauce to crab and artichokes. Put in 9x13 baking dish and sprinkle with cheese.

Bake at 350° for 30 minutes. Sprinkle with paprika before serving.

My nephew remembers stuffed pork that I occasionally did.

STUFFED PORK

1 boneless double loin pork roast (4 to 5 lbs.), the two parts tied together so that the spread goes in the middle.

½ c. chopped fresh mushrooms

¼ c. chopped onion

1 Tbsp. olive oil

½ 10-oz. pkg. frozen chopped spinach, thawed (Put the other half in soup pot.)

1 c. soft bread crumbs

Salt and pepper

¼ tsp. sage

⅛ tsp. garlic powder

Cook mushrooms and onions in olive oil. Stir in remaining ingredients (except pork). Cook until spinach is tender.

Separate the loins, spread one with the stuffing, to within an inch of the edges. Top with second loin and tie with string.

Roast uncovered at 325° for 35 minutes per pound. Test with meat thermometer in thickest part of the meat—temperature should be 165°. Let stand to "collect itself" and slice. Serves at least twelve.

Christmas dinner. Who knows what year? And who sent out the memo about red shirts?

The evenings of big Sunday night suppers are gone, and sometimes I am nostalgic for them. But I still like to entertain on Sunday nights. I just usually limit the guests to one couple or at the most two, or sometimes a couple of single friends.

In the late 1970s, a radiologist named Charles Ogilvie came to teach at the Texas College of Osteopathic Medicine, where Joel was on the faculty and where I worked for a couple of years in the community relations office. Charles and his wife, Reva, had a ranch in East Texas where they retreated each weekend. Pretty soon we were invited to visit. At that time, they had one guesthouse on the ranch—two bedrooms and a living-dining-kitchen area. The ranch had several lakes, wooded pathways that Charles had laid out, some cows in the pasture, alligators and fish in the lake. The kids thought it was the best place in the world, and we went back so often that they were disappointed one day to learn that it wasn't our cabin—other people stayed there, too.

While the children fished and dabbled their toes in the water at the small beach area, Reva and I cooked. She was a great, down-home cook, a Missouri farm girl transplanted to Texas. We had huge feasts on the screened-in front porch of their house, looking over the lake at twilight. It's about as close to heaven as I've come.

Charles leased his pastures, since he couldn't care for livestock, but he often kept one feeder calf in a pen not far from the house. One particular calf, however, was so adept at escaping that he was named Houdini. The kids loved him and always stopped to pet him on the way from the main house to our cabin (a good half-mile walk that included making your way across two cattle guards). One night we had beef for dinner—I don't remember what cut or how it was cooked—and Charles asked, "How do you like the meat, kids?" They all chorused that it was great. With a grin, Charles said, "You're eating Houdini." Nobody ate much after that.

The children and I continued to visit the ranch fairly frequently after Joel left. Jamie, in particular, loved it, and he and Melanie and I often went back for weekends, even after they were married. Several years ago my nephew married in Tyler, some thirty miles from the ranch, and the Alters who could attend elected to stay at the ranch. Maddie got to fish for the first time and was excited beyond belief. Sunday morning before we left for home, we all went to The Shed in Edom, a place that holds the memories of happy dinners even if the food isn't that good. I once ordered a chicken salad sandwich and realized that the salad came from Sam's, but the fried catfish and the homemade pies were not to be beat.

Here are some of Reva's recipes that I treasure—and use often.

REVA'S GOOD BEANS

I fix this as is in spite of my ironclad rule against including green peppers in anything!

1 3-lb.-4-oz. can Ranch Style beans
1 28-oz. can diced tomatoes (or two 14-oz. cans)
1 onion, chopped
½ green pepper, seeded and diced
Drain beans, but do not rinse. Put into crockpot along with other ingredients and simmer all day if you have to. (You can probably get by with less, but it's nice to let them thicken up.)

AUNT REVA'S CHILI RELLEÑOS

2 4-oz. cans whole green chilies

½ lb. sharp cheddar (or as much as you want to use)

5 eggs

¼ c. milk

Grease and butter a pie pan. Spread chilies in a single layer on the pan. Cover with grated cheese. Mix eggs and milk and pour over cheese and chilies. Bake at 325° for 30 minutes or until eggs have set.

REVA'S ASPARAGUS

2 c. asparagus (The recipe called for canned, but I use one bunch of fresh, trimmed and lightly cooked.)

1 c. sour cream

¼ c. mayonnaise

2 Tbsp. lemon juice

Buttered breadcrumbs

This actually doesn't come with directions, but Reva used to lay the asparagus, fan-shaped, in a pie plate. For easier serving, I put it in single layer in a small rectangular baking dish. Mix sour cream, mayonnaise, and lemon juice and pour over asparagus. Top with breadcrumbs and bake until topping is brown and dish is heated through.

Reva and I had a running disagreement about what she called "sheath cake," which I contended made no sense. It's a *sheet* cake, because it's made in a sheet pan—or at least a jelly roll pan, which is a sheet pan of sorts. Be sure to read the directions, because this goes together like no cake I ever heard of.

SHEET CAKE

2 sticks butter or margarine

4 Tbsp. cocoa

1 c. water.

Bring these ingredients to a boil and add:

2 c. sugar

2 c. flour

Mix and add:

 2 eggs

1 tsp. vanilla

½ c. buttermilk

1 tsp. baking soda

Mix and bake in a greased rimmed cookie sheet at 400° for 20 minutes.

Separately combine in saucepan:

1 stick butter

4 Tbsp. cocoa

6 Tbsp. milk

Bring to a boil and add:

1 lb. powdered sugar

1 c. chopped nuts

1 tsp. vanilla

Spread over hot cake.

Reva also gave me a recipe that I make every time I have a tree-trimming party. It's really the same ingredients as chocolate chip cookies, just put together in a different way. I love it.

TOFFEE BARS

½ lb. (2 sticks) butter

1 c. brown sugar

1 egg yolk

2 c. flour

1 tsp. vanilla

12 oz. semisweet chocolate chips

1 c. chopped pecans

Preheat oven to 350° and grease a 9x13 pan.

Cream butter and sugar. Add the egg yolk and beat. Sift in the flour and then add the vanilla. Spread the batter in the pan—it will be difficult to cover all the corners and you'll have a thick batter that you will probably have to spread by hand, and then it will be thinly distributed. Bake for 25 minutes.

Take the cake out of the oven, cover it with chocolate chips, and return to the oven for three minutes. When you remove it from the oven this time, smooth the chocolate evenly with the blade of a table knife and sprinkle with nuts. Cool.

Makes about thirty pieces, depending on how you cut them.

After Charles retired, he and Reva ran the ranch as a guest ranch. The cabins were booked for weekends in advance, and they hosted huge picnics for groups, particularly biking groups, because biking became Charles' passion. But guests in the cabins always found breakfast waiting on their kitchen counter when they checked in. Reva would provide rolls or a loaf of special bread, orange juice, coffee makings, and so on. One of her prize recipes was for prune bread, and she would share it with no one. I know—I asked for it. But when I told Charles that I was doing this book, he said, "I can get that recipe for you." So here's my posthumous tribute to Reva, her devoted friendship, and all those great meals I had at her table.

PRUNE BREAD WITH APRICOTS

2 c. sugar

1 c. vegetable oil

1 tsp. each cinnamon, nutmeg, and allspice

1 c. prunes and 1 cup dried apricots, cooked together in boiling water until soft (there should be one cup of cooked fruit)

1 c. buttermilk mixed with 1 tsp. baking soda

1 c. nuts, either walnuts or pecans, chopped

2¼ c. flour

Mix well. Cook one hour in two loaf pans.

Reva preferred to mix dry ingredients together and mix alternately with liquids. Add the buttermilk last.

As a single parent, I didn't date much—not that I didn't want to. But most men in my age bracket—I was then in my forties—saw four young children as a great liability. And I didn't meet many men who I thought would love my children as much as I did. (I met a few who wanted to discipline the children their way, and I was having none of that.) I saw women in my situation and of my age who were so hell-bent on their own happiness that their children suffered. I didn't want that. I honestly dated only one man who would have loved my children and loved raising them—he had been raised by a stepfather—but it didn't work out for other reasons. If by remote chance he ever reads this—he is long gone from my life and from Texas, and maybe from this world—he should know I still think of him.

One night I fixed him chicken piccata—a poor man's version of veal piccata—and I remember he said, in his southern drawl, "Bless your heart, you bought boneless chicken!" That told me that no one had ever bought him boneless chicken before, and I wondered even more about his previous life.

CHICKEN PICCATA

4 boneless chicken breast halves

1 egg

1 Tbsp. milk

Flour

Cornmeal

4 Tbsp. butter

Juice of ½ lemon

½ cup water

Chicken bouillon cube

Mix milk and egg in a shallow bowl; mix flour and cornmeal in a second bowl.

Pound chicken until it's as flat as you can get it—¼ inch is the goal.

Dip breasts in egg mixture and then in flour/cornmeal mixture.

Melt butter in skillet over medium heat. Sauté chicken breasts until browned on both sides, adding more butter if necessary. Remove to platter when browned and cooked through.

Reduce heat. Add lemon juice to skillet. Add water slowly (no more than ¾ c. total) and a chicken bouillon cube. Stir to loosen browned bits from bottom of skillet and melt bouillon cube. Return meat to skillet and cook five minutes until warmed through.

Serve with thin lemon slices and chopped parsley for garnish.

Another thing I remember serving that particular man is a broccoli chicken casserole. I got the recipe from a neighbor.

CHICKEN DIVAN

2 10-oz. pkgs. frozen broccoli spears

¼ c. butter or margarine

6 Tbsp. flour

½ tsp. salt

Dash of pepper

2 c. chicken broth

½ c. whipping cream

3 Tbsp. white wine

3 chicken breasts, halved and cooked

¼ c. Parmesan cheese

Cook broccoli and drain.

Melt butter and blend in the flour, along with salt and pepper.

Add chicken broth and cook until mixture thickens and bubbles. Stir in cream and wine.

Place broccoli crosswise in a 12x7½x2 dish. Pour half the sauce over. Top with chicken and pour remaining sauce over it. Top with Parmesan. Bake at 350° for 10 minutes or until heated through. Then broil till sauce is golden, about 5 minutes. Serves six.

But I found one thing that sure sparked a single girl's social life: I began to write restaurant reviews. I reviewed for a magazine then published by the Fort Worth Chamber of Commerce and also for the *Dallas Business Press*. The latter was more fun because they let me pick the restaurants; our understanding was that if I did four or five moderately priced establishments in a row, I could then splurge on an upscale restaurant. So one night I took Uncle Bob to a new French restaurant that had opened in a charming old frame house. I have no idea what we had for dinner, but it was delicious. The bill came to a hundred dollars (in the mid-1980s, I considered that a lot), but he pushed back from the table and announced loudly, "I'm still hungry." So much for Continental portions.

Reviewing for the chamber folks was a little less adventuresome. They made the assignments, and I couldn't say anything bad about the food because they only assigned restaurants that had joined the chamber and therefore couldn't be insulted. Not exactly what I'd call reviewing, but it was still free dinners. One night I took Alan Burk, an old buddy and the son of my real-estate friend, to a restaurant that had opened in a house once occupied by 1920s gangsters—there were gun slits or whatever as proof of its wayward days. The food was awful. I remember Alan poking at his chicken and saying, "Look! A rubber duckie!" But I couldn't say that, so I wrote about the history of the house.

In those years, before Jamie could drive and therefore date, he was my best dinner date. One night, with Jamie in tow, I reviewed a restaurant called The Village House. The owners were warm, welcoming, and friendly; the food, Armenian in origin, was terrific. I remember particularly an appetizer platter and a spinach-and-beef dish. I raved so much in my review that the restaurant's business picked up a lot. Every time the owners asked people how they heard about their place, the answer was my review. In gratitude, the owner appeared at my front door that Christmas with a huge gift package of dried fruit. Jamie and I went back to The Village House from time to time and were always treated like royalty. But one night it had simply vanished. We were crushed.

With the new cuisine that surrounds us—all those peppers and chilies and the pan-Asia cooking—I'm not sure my skills are up to reviewing anymore. But it was fun—and it was a good outlet for a mom who was homebound a lot.

Prince Charming may not have come along during those years, but I made a lot of new friends—a variety of people I would never have known if I'd stayed in the rather constricted social life of a doctor's wife, at least as I'd known that life. At a Christmas party recently, a woman I know casually from church said, "You have the nicest friends of anyone I know."

"I do," I said. "Why don't you come to tree-trimming and meet fifty or sixty of them?"

The other big thing that happened during the casserole years was that while raising children and cooking, cooking, cooking, I found my career. I went to work part time at TCU as coordinator of community classes. For reasons too complicated to explain, the director-to-be of TCU Press, the academic book publishing arm of the university, was parked in my office while waiting for the current director to retire. (They did not get along.) We became friends, and one day he looked at me and said, "You want to be the editor?"

"Sure," I said. That was my job interview.

For two or three months, I was both coordinator of community classes and editor of the press—and then we moved into the press's office, and I became editor, still on a three-quarter-time basis. I loved it and knew I had found the work I'd been looking for. In 1986, the director left to take over SMU Press, and I became acting director. It took a year and a half for me to get the permanent title, because there was always a move afoot to close the press. But that never happened, and in 1987 I got the title.

In the '90s, the kids were still mostly at home—except Megan, who left as quickly after college as she could, moving to Austin to become a legislative assistant and later go to law school. But they were grown; they had their own cars; they kept their own hours, with some oversight on my part. There was, for instance, the night Colin came home at 5 A.M. and I greeted him in the driveway wearing the T-shirt I slept in (or tried to sleep). Imagine my horror when he said not to worry—he'd been swimming in a quarry. Ye gods!

But freed from the intensity of raising children, I did some of my best writing and produced three of the four novels that I think are my most interesting. I had found my niche in writing about women of the American West, and I fictionalized the lives of Libby Custer, Jessie Benton Frémont, Lucille Mulhall (the first woman trick roper to ride in Buffalo Bill's West), and finally Etta Place, girlfriend of the Sundance Kid and a participating member of the famed Hole-In-The-Wall Gang. The vogue for such novels has passed, but I found another niche. As early as the 1980s I began writing juvenile nonfiction on assignment for companies that published for school libraries. I've written so many of those that when someone asks how many books I've published, I say, "About sixty," and then hasten to explain that many of them are thirty- or forty-page books for children. Lots of research, yes, but not a lot of writing. Most non-writers say, "A book is a book."

The years of children were also the years during which I finally felt I could call myself an author. I used to say the children would put on my gravestone: "I remember her. She always said, 'Go on now, I'm busy,' or 'Hurry on!' " But they were wonderful years that I wouldn't trade for anything, and I think—hope—the children feel that way, too.

Chapater IV

Living Alone and Liking It–
Well, Most of the Time

While raising my family, I moved several times—Megan used to say, "Mom gets bored every few years, and we move." First we left that big, two-story house that had been my dream home but, by the time we left, was a terrible upkeep burden. We went to a charming 1920s brick with arched windows, inlaid wood floors, and no family room, although it did have four bedrooms and an enclosed porch that provided an office for me. But if the kids, as teenagers, wanted friends over and I did too at the same time, we had no open areas.

We moved to a rambling, three-bedroom 1960s ranch-style, the newest house I've ever lived in, where the boys lived in the converted attached garage. It was great for parties—mine and theirs. One night for some perverse reason when they were well grown, Jamie and Jordan regaled me with tales of the parties they'd given while I was out of town on business. More than I wanted to know!

But I saw the handwriting on the wall. Megan lived in the dorm or shared a house with girls while she was at TCU, and six months after graduation, she moved to Austin permanently. The boys would surely go soon, and Jordan and I would be alone. I needed a house where I had "control of my space"—not one where, from my bedroom, I had not the faintest clue what was happening at the other end of the house.

Back to the neighborhood of charming, older homes—this one a red brick with three bedrooms, an interesting floor plan, a family room, a guest house, and a wonderful, huge front porch. But no one left. In fact, Melanie moved in with us. The boys lived in the garage apartment, and whoever else was around stayed in the house.

Jamie and Melanie went first, but only to Dallas. Of course, I thought they'd come home for Sunday supper, which didn't happen. Still, they weren't too far away. Then Colin went to Grand Cayman Island to run a small dive hotel. That was too far, and I watched unhappily about 5:30 one morning as a friend drove him to the airport. Then I went inside and cried.

When Jordan moved to Aspen, Colorado—was that before or after she moved to an apartment?—I surprised myself by suddenly breaking into tears at odd moments for days. Aspen didn't work out, and Jordan moved in and out several times over the years. But we became like ships that pass in the night, rarely home at the same time. I eased into living alone.

Friends predicted that I was so involved with my family and so used to having all those rowdy kids and their friends around that I wouldn't handle living alone well. I think I've surprised them. I love it when kids come home, but when they leave, my Australian shepherd Scooby, my big fluffy tomcat Wynona (don't ask about the name!), and I breathe a sigh of relief that we've got our house back.

Oh, sometimes I wish for a companion—I told a good friend that when everyone had gone home after four days of festivities for the wedding of Jordan and Christian, I longed for someone to sit and relive it with. She, happily married, replied: "You could have called me. It'd be a lot easier than having a man around." Another time I announced that I needed to find a husband so I didn't keep getting short shrift on sleeping arrangements when we were all together. The same friend suggested that I consider a traveling companion instead.

Mine is not a solitary existence, in spite of living alone. I fill the house with people frequently. The Alter clan still has family dinners—we can make an occasion out of anything, but we most often gather for birthdays.

These days, we can't always get the whole family together, though no one would miss a major holiday.

I've found some new recipes I cook, like the Easter that I fixed strawberry salsa for an appetizer and served a great potato casserole with the ham. (I'm intrigued by fruit salsas, and there are a lot of recipes out there—check www.epicurious.com for watermelon salsa.)

STRAWBERRY SALSA

1 pint chopped strawberries

8 green onions

2 pints cherry tomatoes, chopped

¼ c. fresh cilantro, chopped

Mix together. Coat with a dressing made of:

6 Tbsp. olive oil

2 Tbsp. balsamic vinegar

Pinch of salt

Refrigerate at least an hour. Serve with tortilla chips.

Christian told me that he serves this casserole when he gives breakfasts for clients. His father won't eat onions, and I couldn't convince him that he wouldn't taste the onions in this. They just enrich the flavor.

POTATO CASSEROLE

2 lbs. frozen hash browns, thawed

1 can cream of chicken soup

2 c. grated cheddar

½ c. chopped onions

½ c. softened margarine

¼ tsp. each salt and pepper

1 16-oz. carton sour cream

Mix all together, being sure to add the sour cream last. Place in a buttered 9x13 casserole.

Topping

2 c. crushed Corn Flakes

¼ c. margarine or butter, melted

Mix Corn Flakes with margarine or butter. Sprinkle over potato mixture. Bake 45 minutes at 350°. This could feed Cox's army—I have halved it for four to six, and it works fine. (Yeah, a lot of cholesterol, but it's so good.)

Jordan loves Caesar salad, and I found a recipe purported to be the original from Caesar Cardini of Tijuana, who invented the salad when the power went off at his hotel and he had to feed his guests with what he had on hand. Originally it was not a tossed salad as we know it today, but a finger food—the dressing was spread on individual leaves of romaine, which the diner picked up and ate one by one.

CAESAR SALAD

1 anchovy fillet, smashed

3 Tbsp. grated Parmesan

2 Tbsp. mayonnaise

2 tsp. fresh lemon juice

½ tsp. Dijon mustard

1 clove garlic, smashed

¼ tsp. Worcestershire

¼ c. olive oil

2 heads romaine

Fresh Parmesan shavings

Croutons (preferably homemade with olive oil, garlic and bread baked in cubes in a medium oven until brown).

Combine dressing ingredients with whisk. Spread romaine leaves on platter; pour dressing over, being sure to leave clean lettuce at the base of each leaf so that diners can pick up it up to eat—finger food at its best! Sprinkle with croutons and top with fresh Parmesan shavings.

Christmas in Santa Fe, looking our worst. Maddie was the only grandchild, and Christian hadn't appeared on the scene yet.

During their courtship and early marriage, Jordan and Christian did much of their entertaining by giving big parties on my front porch, always on a night when I could be part of the fun. One of her friends said, "I'd never miss Mexican night on the Alter front porch."

My front porch is a comfortable place—an antique couch (chained to the concrete), a barbecue (also chained), a mesh table with four rocking chairs (cabled together—ah, the times we live in!), and lots of pots of herbs and plants. I don't go in for flowering plants much because of a northern exposure, but I do have flowering plants in the beds in front of the house. And for some time I had a bottle tree. When Melanie first saw it, she thought someone (one of my own children) had pranked me good. It took me a while to convince her it was deliberate. Then there was the day that Colin poked fun at my cheap habit of drinking box wine by putting an empty box on one of the limbs! The bottle tree fell apart, and since the garden was filling in, I gave it up.

But back to Mexican night: Jordan browns hamburger meat and adds taco seasoning, chops scallions and tomatoes, grates cheese, puts out sour cream, salsa and chips, and taco or chalupa shells, and everyone builds his or her own dinner. Sometimes I do some brownies for dessert. It's the menu she's requested for her birthday dinner for years. Not fancy, but fun. As her thirty-first birthday approached, she asked for the same dinner on the porch—with a cast of close to twenty.

Occasionally she's scheduled a happy hour gathering, but her friends have been known to arrive for happy hour and stay until 10:00 or so. A favorite dip then is the standard onion soup one. Other girls bring various dips. Now that Jordan and Christian have Jacob, that pattern has changed. But then, there's a portable crib for the baby in the guest room—and a grand playroom that he and his cousins love.

Jordan and Christian eat with me fairly frequently, and I've learned to cook for Christian, who has been previously identified as "vegetable-impaired." His mother told me she used to cook four separate meals—one for each family member—and when she finally sat down to eat her supper, the others had finished. Christian likes green beans vinaigrette and the German potato salad I do.

CHRISTIAN'S GREEN BEANS

3 slices bacon, cooked and crumbled, grease saved

3 scallions, chopped

Vinegar to taste

1 28-oz. can green beans, drained

Fry bacon and remove from the skillet to drain on paper towels. Leave enough grease in the skillet to sauté scallions. Pour in vinegar to taste, and add drained green beans. Crumble the bacon over the beans. Serve hot.

One night I roasted a large chicken for Jordan and Christian and had so much left that I thought I'd never eat it up.

ROAST CHICKEN WITH LEMON AND THYME

1 roasting chicken

1 lemon, peel grated to make 2 tsp.

5 cloves garlic

2 Tbsp. fresh thyme or 1 tsp. dried

1 Tbsp. olive oil

½ c. white wine

2 Tbsp. butter

1 c. chicken broth

Rinse chicken thoroughly and pat dry; be sure to remove inner parts, neck, etc.

Mix garlic, crushed fresh or dried thyme, lemon peel, and olive oil. Rub thoroughly all over chicken. Quarter the lemon and stick in the cavity. Tie legs and roast, with meat thermometer in thickest part of thigh, until it reaches 180°.

Loosen pan drippings with white wine (use more if necessary); pour off wine and reserve. Put butter in the pan, heat, and stir. Return wine to pan and stir until thickened. Add chicken broth (or bouillon from a cube). Stir until thickened.

Cool chicken before carving.

I recently found a recipe on the Web that I wished I'd had when all the kids were home. I never made meatballs because frying them was so much trouble. But these are easy, and I made stroganoff out of them, which the newlyweds loved.

MEATBALLS

2 lb. lean ground beef

2 eggs, lightly beaten

1 c. dry bread crumbs

¼ c. Parmesan, grated, not the flaked kind

2 tsp. garlic powder

Mix and shape into 48 meatballs, about an inch each. Bake on lightly greased cooking sheet at 400° for 20 minutes.

You can just throw these in the freezer in batches of however many you think you might use at a time.

MEATBALL STROGANOFF

1 medium onion, chopped
1 c. sliced mushrooms
½ stick butter.
¼ c. flour
¼ c. ketchup
2 14½ oz. cans beef broth
1 8-oz. pkg. cream cheese
Sauté onion in butter; add mushrooms and cook until soft. Stir in
flour. Add ketchup, broth, and cream cheese. Add about 24 meatballs from the recipe above. Mix lightly and heat through until cream
cheese melts. Serve over egg noodles.

MEATBALL SANDWICH

Eating alone? These are great again. Pull four meatballs out of the
freezer, along with a sub sandwich roll. (I always have various breads,
lots of them in the freezer, leftovers from various occasions.) I don't
like too much bread, so I hollow out some, then add meatballs, cover
with ½ c. prepared spaghetti sauce (freeze the rest), and top with pro-
volone and the top of the sandwich. Brown on slow heat in skillet. (To
make the bread into panini, find a brick, wash it thoroughly, and wrap
in double layer of heavy duty foil; as the sandwich fries—3 minutes on
a side or thereabouts—weigh it down with the brick. Presto, panini!)

When Colin and Lisa first returned from the Caribbean, they lived with
Lisa's parents in Sugar Land, Texas. Lisa's mother, Torhild, was born and
raised in Norway and came to this country as a soldier's bride at the age of
seventeen. She still cooks some of the dishes she knew as a child, and Colin
particularly fell in love with these hamburgers (and I might add, with John
and Torhild, as did we all). Torhild calls them Norwegian meat cakes, but
we've all come to use the term *hamburger*. I can't believe they used pack-
aged gravy mix when she was young—I think that's an American shortcut
she has introduced!

NORWEGIAN HAMBURGERS

3-4 slices of onion

3 Tbsp. butter (do not use oil)

1½ lbs. extra-lean hamburger (extra-lean is important)

2 eggs

3 Tbsp. cornstarch or potato starch

½ tsp. pepper

Milk as needed

4-5 envelopes instant gravy mix, prepared as directed

2 beef bullion cubes

Sauté onion in butter. Mix hamburger, eggs, cornstarch and pepper. Add milk as needed; start with ¼ c. and add ¼ c. at a time, but DON'T let the meat mixture get soggy. The last time I made a double batch of these, they tended to fall apart while I was browning them. I bet my mom's trick of throwing a little tapioca into meatloaf would work here, too. Shape into patties and brown in same skillet as onions. Remove. Make gravy in skillet, according to package directions. Add 2 bouillon cubes. When gravy thickens, return burgers and onions to pan and simmer 45 to 60 minutes.

Serve with white rice, egg noodles, or boiled potatoes. Peas, beets, or green beans are nice with this.

I'd always sort of avoided pesto. The few times I tried it, I didn't think I liked it. But one year I had a luxurious pot of basil. It was November, and the threat of a frost was imminent, even when the temperature climbed back into the 80s. (Ah, Texas!) So I decided I couldn't possibly waste all that basil.

I was besieged with several recipes, including a Weight Watchers one that called for water. I couldn't quite do that. This is what I did:

PESTO

2 large cloves garlic

2 c. loosely packed basil leaves

2 Tbsp. ground pecans

2 tsp. lemon or lime juice

2 Tbsp. parmesan

2 tsp. salt

½ tsp. black pepper

⅔ c. good olive oil

Process garlic and basil until finely chopped. Add remaining ingredients except olive oil and process until smooth. Then, with motor still running, add olive oil.

I tossed it over pasta, cooked potatoes, and fresh green beans, and it was great. I've now begun to add it when I cook green noodles. And I often make an appetizer with pesto.

A big pesto hint: pour it into cubes in an ice cube tray. When frozen, pop the cubes loose, throw in a bag, and store in the freezer. One cube is enough to cover a small brick of cream cheese, flavor a pasta dish, or do all kinds of other things.

CREAM CHEESE AND PESTO

1 8-oz. block cream cheese

1 frozen cube pesto, defrosted

One pkg. crescent rolls

1 egg, beaten

Split block of cream cheese horizontally. Cover one layer with 2 Tbsp. pesto and top with second layer of cream cheese.

Unroll package of crescent rolls and press the seams together to make a rectangle.

Put the cream cheese in the middle and wrap with the dough. Brush with beaten egg and bake for 15 minutes at 350°. Serve with crackers, baguette slices, or whatever you have. Serves twelve (maybe).

I like to entertain at breakfast—or brunch, if you prefer. It seems to me a sociable hour. Of course, you have to choose the day, preferably a Sunday when everyone's relaxed and not feeling the need to rush off somewhere. (Okay, you can skip church one week.) The day after Jordan's huge wedding, I served breakfast to twenty people. Many of my friends asked, "Why did you do that?" But the guests were the out-of-town friends I loved and wouldn't see again for a while. It wasn't that hard.

The menu? Egg casseroles, fruit salad, a spiral-cut ham, and assorted fruit breads. I cheated and got the casseroles from a local restaurant the day before, not realizing that I'd have to bake them and they'd take twice as long as they told me—have another Bloody Mary, everyone!

The ham, of course, came straight from the market, and the breads were in my freezer—persimmon bread from a good friend, pumpkin bread from Megan, and a cranberry-orange-dried apricot bread I'd made and frozen. I made the salad the day before and had the coffee ready to plug in, plus a jug of orange juice in the fridge, along with Bloody Mary mix and a son-in-law who's handy about mixing it. I served it all on disposable dishes and flatware.

FRUIT SALAD

   1 lb. thawed strawberries, sliced
   ¼-½ c. sugar, to taste
   8 oz. pineapple chunks
   1 can apricot pie filling, or flavor of your choice
   2-3 bananas
   In a large bowl (preferably one with a lid), put strawberries. Add sugar
   to taste—not too much. Add pineapple chunks and apricot pie filling.
   Chill. Just before you serve it, add bananas, cut in chunks.
   Feeds at least twelve people. (I ate it for days after the wedding, when I
   had made a double batch!)

Now that my children are grown and gone to homes of their own, they like to make a ceremony out of breakfast when we're all together, no matter whose house we're visiting. It's always scrambled eggs and bacon—and maybe some hash browns. But we can never agree on the eggs; Colin and I like ours scrambled with cottage cheese instead of milk (it gives them great body and depth), a practice that brings loud expressions of horror from everyone else in the family. I also like mine soft-scrambled, while the girls like hard little bricks of eggs, so that I am always scrambling to unscramble my eggs before they turn to concrete. Brandon searches the icebox desperately for Tabasco, salsa, anything hot to spice up his eggs, and Jamie says eggs don't really do it for him.

I used to fix little skillet sausages (easier than bacon), but they all prefer bacon, so I do huge batches of it, always crisp. I do it on a broiler pan in the oven. (Mel wraps bacon

Jordan and me at a porch party.

in paper towels and does it in the microwave in small batches—three minutes at medium for three pieces. You have to get good bacon—cheap stuff will stick to the towels.)

The first time I ever met Brandon's parents, I was to serve brunch to them. They were to be in Fort Worth for the wedding of a friend of B's. Ahead of time I said to Megan and B that I had a wonderful chicken-chili cheesecake recipe that I had served at a brunch for some friends after a Texas Institute of Letters meeting, and it was well received. Brandon was absolutely horrified and said he was sure his dad would prefer those eggs that I made with a tomato sauce.

RANCH EGGS

½ lb. bacon, cooked until crisp and set aside; 3 Tbsp. drippings reserved

1 tomato, coarsely chopped

4 green onions, sliced

Clove of garlic

½ tsp. chili powder

Salt (Be careful—tomato sauce is salty.)

8-oz. can tomato sauce

12 eggs

Enough milk to scramble eggs (or cottage cheese, sour cream, whatever you prefer)

Mix everything (except bacon, eggs, and milk or whatever) and simmer. Separately in skillet, with bacon drippings, scramble eggs. Add a little more salt and pepper. Serve eggs topped with sauce and bacon, broken into bits. Pass tortillas.

I don't care what Brandon thought—that chicken-chili cheesecake is good, although it's a bit of work and also pretty high-fat, with all that cream cheese.

CHICKEN-CHILI CHEESECAKE

1½ c. crushed tortilla chips

¼ c. butter, melted

3 8-oz. pkgs. cream cheese, softened

4 large eggs

1 tsp. chili powder

1 tsp. Worcestershire

Pinch of salt

1½ c. cooked chicken, shredded

2 4-oz. cans chopped green chilies, drained

6 oz. shredded Monterrey Jack cheese

1 16-oz. container sour cream

1 tsp. seasoned salt

6 sliced green onions

Picante sauce

Mix tortilla chips and butter and use to line bottom and one inch of the sides of a 9-inch closed spring-form pan.

Beat cream cheese until light and fluffy. Beating as you go, add eggs, one at a time. Stir in chili powder, Worcestershire, and salt. Pour half the mixture into the spring-form pan. Cover with chicken, chilies, Monterrey Jack, and scallions. Pour remaining cream cheese on top. Bake at 350° for 10 minutes; then reduce heat to 300° and bake until set (at least an hour—test it with a knife; when the knife comes out clean, it's set). Cool on wire rack.

Mix sour cream and seasoned salt and use to ice the cooled cheesecake. Chill overnight. Decorate with sliced green onions and picante sauce.

Sometimes the Book Ladies, a group of ladies whose careers revolve around books and who meet once a month for breakfast, meet in private homes. One time when I had them to my house, with Bobbie to help, I served a glorified version of pancakes.

PANCAKE BANANA SPLITS

1 pkg. frozen pancakes

3 bananas

1 small carton strawberry yogurt

1 small carton vanilla yogurt

1 small can crushed pineapple

Frozen blueberries

Granola

Fresh strawberries

Microwave pancakes, according to package directions. (Don't overheat them so that they become tough.) Quarter bananas, cutting in half lengthwise and then each half in half.

Put two pancakes on each plate. Top with banana pieces, add a dollop each of strawberry and vanilla yogurt, a spoonful of pineapple, and blueberries. Sprinkle with granola and garnish with sliced strawberries.

Makes four servings. Double or triple for a crowd.

I haven't served these for a long time, but they were good in the casserole years, and I'm about ready to try them again. You have to start the day before.

RICE FRITTERS

Rice to make 1½ c., following the directions on the package.
1 pkg. dried yeast
½ c. lukewarm water
Pinch of sugar
3 eggs
1½ c. flour
½ tsp. each salt and sugar
Pinch of nutmeg
Vegetable oil for frying
Cinnamon/sugar mixture, equal parts

The night before serving, cook rice until all moisture is absorbed. While it's hot, mash the rice with the back of a wooden spoon. Let it cool until it's lukewarm. Meanwhile, dissolve a package of dried yeast in lukewarm water—add pinch of sugar to hasten the rising action. Stir the yeast into the rice and let it stand on the counter, covered, overnight.

In the morning, stir together eggs, flour, salt, sugar, and nutmeg. Stir into the rice; cover and let it rise in a warm place for about 30 minutes. Make fritters by dropping teaspoonfuls of batter into deep hot oil. Fry until golden brown, drain, and serve sprinkled with powdered sugar or a cinnamon/sugar mixture. Makes about two dozen.

These aren't good for a crowd, because you can really only make two at a time, and most people can eat a whole one. But they are so good!

BANANA CREPES

3 eggs

⅔ c. flour

¼ tsp. salt

1 Tbsp. sugar

½ c. milk

4 Tbsp. butter, melted

1 tsp. grated lemon peel

⅓ c. butter

⅓ c. brown sugar

⅓ c. orange juice

3 bananas, sliced

Beat eggs in a bowl; separately sift flour, salt, and sugar; combine milk, melted butter, and lemon peel. Add dry ingredients to eggs alternately with the milk mixture.

Heat oven to 400°. Put 1 tsp. butter in each of two cake pans and heat in oven for 5 minutes (watch that it doesn't scorch—I sometimes think that's too long). Divide batter between pans and bake 18 to 20 minutes. Meanwhile, mix remaining butter with brown sugar, orange juice, and bananas and heat until butter and sugar are melted.

Slide crepes onto plates. Cover one half of each with sauce and fold other half over like an omelet. Messy but good.

To me, eggs Benedict—or better yet, eggs Florentine (on a bed of spinach)—is the classiest breakfast dish you can serve people. I have an almost sure-fire hollandaise sauce that I use for that (as well as for serving whole artichokes, broccoli, etc.).

HOLLANDAISE SAUCE
  3 egg yolks
  Juice of 1 lemon
  Dash of cayenne
  1 stick butter
  In food processor (I love my counter-size small one for such things)
  blend egg yolks, lemon juice, and cayenne. Melt butter and pour into
  processor. (Mine doesn't have a pour spout, so I dump it all in.) Blend,
  pour into saucepan, and heat medium high. Stir constantly until
  thickened. Remove from heat immediately. Theoretically, the sauce is
  supposed to thicken when you pour the hot butter over the eggs and
  blend it, but that never works for me.

A final word on breakfasts: I'm no good at omelets; I love to eat them
elsewhere (Kerbey Lane Café in Austin) but never try them myself.

I used to think that when I retired, I'd take a professional chef's course—
a real one where you wear a uniform and toque and learn to use good
knives and make a roux and all that kind of thing. But I decided that was
too much time and too much standing on my feet and not as much fun as
I was having cooking for family and friends. Besides, when I semi-retired,
I ended up teaching two freshman English seminars and having less time
than before. I don't have time, even in retirement, to become a chef—or a
gourmet cook.

In the meantime, I cook for friends a lot. I love to have small dinner
parties. Mostly, I cook something new every time I entertain—I like the
experimentation—but I do repeat a couple of recipes.

The first time a friend had this leg of lamb, she e-mailed me the next day
and offered me $8,000 for the recipe.

$8,000 LEG OF LAMB WITH VEGETABLES
  About 5 white-skinned potatoes, peeled and sliced
  3 onions, thinly sliced

3 tomatoes, thinly sliced
Salt and pepper
Dried thyme
Chopped garlic to taste
¾ c. white wine
⅓ c. vegetable oil
6-7-lb. leg of lamb, excess fat trimmed but bone in
The whole thing that makes this good is that the lamb juices drip into the vegetables, making them taste incredible. Grease a 9x13 pan and layer the bottom with sliced potatoes. Add onions and then tomatoes. Sprinkle each layer with salt, pepper, dried thyme, and a little chopped garlic. Pour white wine and vegetable oil over the vegetables. Cover pan with a cake or oven rack.
Season lamb to taste with salt and pepper and set it on the cake rack. Roast at 400° until meat thermometer registers 145° (about 75 minutes—the lamb will be medium rare; roast longer for better done, but don't overdo it!). Turn the lamb every 20 minutes or so and baste with liquids from the vegetables. Remove from oven and let it collect itself before carving.

This dish is more complicated, but Jordan likes it so well that one year she and Christian spent New Year's Eve with me so they could have a fancy dinner. The requested menu was roulade. This mixes pork, chicken, and prosciutto.

ROULADE
1 pork tenderloin (If you can have the butcher butterfly it and pound it into a rectangle, with the meat about ⅓ inch thick, you'll save yourself a lot of work.)
3 chicken breasts halves, pounded flat
3 oz. paper-thin prosciutto
Salt and pepper
Olive oil

Sauce:

2 tsp. crushed green peppercorns

4 garlic cloves, mashed

2 c. fresh parsley, chopped

2 tsp. dried basil

4 tsp. olive oil

½ 2-oz. can flat anchovy fillets, drained (Don't cheat and leave out the anchovies because you don't like them—they make a huge difference, and the taste isn't fishy.)

Mix sauce ingredients.

Spread pork on work surface; cover with one third of the sauce. Top with chicken breasts, evenly spread over the pork, and top with half the remaining sauce. Cover with prosciutto and then remaining sauce. Starting at the long side of the rectangle, roll the meats into a tight roll and tie with string. You can do this the day before you serve it.

Season the meat roll with salt and pepper and brown all sides in hot olive oil. Remove from skillet and wrap in heavy-duty foil, sealing tightly. Put on a lipped baking sheet (in case it drips) and bake about 50 minutes at 400°.

If you want, you can make gravy. (The meat is so good that I'm not sure it always needs it.) You might just use chicken broth and butter. The original recipe called for bacon, chicken broth, heavy cream, flour and butter. I'd rather avoid the heavy cream, and just mix chicken broth and a bit of butter. If you need to thicken it, use cornstarch in cold water.

Remove string from roulade. Slice, and pass sauce with it. Great with mashed potatoes.

I don't cook much veal, but this is a particularly good recipe.

VEAL SCALOPINI ON PUREE OF GREEN PEAS

¾ c. finely chopped shallots

2 c. frozen petite peas, thawed

¾ c. chicken broth

1 tsp. tarragon

Salt and pepper

6 3-oz. boneless veal round cutlets, cut into three pieces

Spray a nonstick skillet with vegetable oil spray and heat over medium heat. Add shallots. Sauté about a minute. Add peas and sauté for two minutes. Add chicken broth Boil quickly and remove from heat. Allow to cool slightly and put in food processor. Add tarragon. Puree until smooth. Season with salt and pepper, tasting first since the broth may make it salty already.

Pound veal between wax paper until it's as thin as you can get it—¼ inch is good. Sprinkle with salt and pepper. Spray nonstick skillet and heat over medium high heat. Sauté veal quickly until golden brown and just cooked through, putting only a few pieces in the pan at a time. (These will cook quickly, so watch them closely.) Re-warm the peas in saucepan on stove or microwave. Spoon peas onto plates; top with veal.

Serves six.

Two of my publishing friends often come to visit, and we have a pajama party like teenagers. Gayla is marketing director at Texas A&M University Press, and Fran, from Dallas, is a retired director of the University of North Texas Press. We talk about staying up late and drinking lots of wine, but truth be told, we're too old—a couple of glasses of wine, maybe three, and we're asleep before ten. But the visiting and exchange of publishing news and gossip is great.

There's a ritual to these visits. Gayla arrives from College Station in time to go to Central Market (a high-end grocery chain, owned by H-E-B groceries and found in Austin, Houston, and the Dallas/Fort Worth metroplex) with me. We wander and decide what we want for dinner as we shop.

When we get home, Fran is usually waiting in the driveway. Then they gather in the kitchen while I cook. Last time they were here, I fixed a classic Coquille St. Jacques, although I didn't serve it in a scalloped shell dish (I have one my mother gave me), and I didn't pipe it with mashed potatoes in the traditional presentation.

The next day we all went to a sales meeting, and someone asked, "Okay, what did you ladies have for dinner last night?" When I said, "Coquille St. Jacques," he said, "God bless you!" He'd never heard of it.

COQUILLE ST. JACQUES MY WAY (FOR FOUR)

¼ c. coarse fresh bread crumbs

¼ c. grated Parmigiano Reggiano

¾ c. white wine

½ c. water

¼ small onion sliced (or three scallions)

½ small bay leaf

¼ tsp. salt

Dash of freshly ground black pepper

½-¾ lb. fresh sea scallops, cut into smaller pieces—or use the smaller bay scalllops

Five or six small mushrooms, cleaned and sliced

4 Tbsp. butter, divided use

¼ c. heavy cream

1 egg yolk

2 tsp. flour

Minced fresh parsley (flat leaf is best)

Preheat oven to 350°. Spread bread crumbs on baking sheet and toast until pale golden. Cool and toss with grated cheese.

Simmer together wine, water, onion, bay leaf, salt, and pepper. Add scallops and heat until just cooked through—3 minutes at the most (you don't want them to get rubbery). Take scallops out and put aside to cool. Reduce cooking liquid to ½ c. and strain to take out onions, bay leaf, etc.

Sauté mushrooms in 1 Tbsp. butter until most of their liquid is evaporated. Season with salt and pepper.

Whisk together cream and egg yolk in small saucepan or heatproof dish.

Separately melt 2 Tbsp. butter; add flour and whisk until thick. Remove from heat and slowly add cooking liquid, stirring until it is well blended and thickened. Pour slowly into cream and egg mixture, whisking constantly. Then pour back into saucepan. Simmer 1 minute. Remove from heat and season with salt and pepper.

In broiler-proof dish, mix scallops and mushroom into sauce. (If you get sloppy drips around edge of pan, clean with a wet paper towel.) Dot with remaining 1 Tbsp. butter and broil until golden. Sprinkle with parsley and serve with a small salad. It's all you need.

As I said before, I don't do meatballs. But these are different because you make large meatballs and bake them first rather than struggling with them in the skillet. The best story about this is the time that Megan was making the dish and it was Brandon's turn that evening to clean the kitchen. When the recipe said to slide the meatballs into the sauce, Megan dumped them all at once. (That's my Megan—she approaches life with vigor and gusto!) Sauce sprayed everywhere—kitchen counter, walls, floor, etc. Just then Brandon walked into the kitchen. Sorry, but what he said is unprintable.

MY FAVORITE MEATBALLS
 About ⅓ loaf of French bread, crust on, cut into large pieces
 1 c. milk
 2 lbs. ground beef
 2 large eggs
 1 medium onion, finely chopped
 ½ c. chopped parsley
 2 tsp. salt
 1 tsp. ground black pepper
 1 tsp. dried summer savory

Flour

2 Tbsp. butter

1½ tsp. olive oil

2 c. red wine

3 c. beef broth

Combine French bread and milk in bowl and let sit until milk is absorbed. Press bread into milk to be sure all is saturated. Meanwhile, mix beef, eggs, onion with seasonings.

Squeeze milk out of bread (throw the milk out) and add bread to meat mixture. Put it in food processor and blend (it will look really pasty and funny, but keep going). Shape in large meatballs about 1¾ inch in diameter. Bake 30 minutes at 350°.

Put flour in a small brown paper lunch bag and put meatballs in, a few at a time, coating them with flour. Shake off excess.

Melt butter with olive oil in skillet and brown meatballs, a few at a time. Add more butter if needed. Put all meatballs back into skillet. Add red wine to skillet with meatballs; bring to boil until reduced by about half. Add beef broth and simmer about 15 minutes to blend the flavors. Taste for salt and pepper.

Serve in skillet, sprinkled with more chopped parsley for decoration. Great with mashed potatoes. Serves six.

Polenta was one of the trendy foods of the '90s, and it's still good in the new century. If you're having vegetarian friends for dinner, it's a great choice. I found a recipe where you add sweet corn to basic polenta and top it with Parmesan.

POLENTA WITH CORN

1 c. yellow cornmeal

1 c. cold water

2 c. canned chicken broth (or that great broth that comes in a carton)

2 c. frozen corn kernels

¼ c. grated Parmigiano Reggiano

Olive oil

Make polenta by whisking together cornmeal and water. Bring chicken broth to boil and add cornmeal mixture all at once. Stir until it is thickened. Add corn and simmer for about 15 minutes. Mix in Parmesan. Spread on an ungreased pie plate and cool.

When ready to serve, brush polenta with olive oil and turn onto a cookie sheet, oiled side down. Brush top with oil and broil until golden (doesn't take very long at all).

Cut into wedges and top with more grated Parmesan. Serve with a mushroom spaghetti sauce (you can use canned or make your own).

MUSHROOM SPAGHETTI SAUCE

1 medium onion, chopped

1 large garlic clove

2 tsp. olive oil

1 tsp. basil

½ tsp. oregano

Pinch of dried crushed red pepper

½ lb. sliced mushrooms

½ c. white wine, divided use

2 14-oz. cans diced tomatoes, undrained

Fresh parsley, chopped

Sauté onion and garlic in olive oil. Add basil, oregano, red pepper, and mushrooms. Add ¼ c. dry white wine and cook until dry. Add another ¼ c. white wine and the tomatoes. Simmer until reduced by half. Garnish with fresh parsley.

Once I invited an old friend whom I hadn't seen for a while to dinner. We were to be joined by his partner and Sheila and her husband, H.G., and Jordan and Christian. I thought I'd splurge and cook the $8,000 leg of lamb, but Lee finally e-mailed to confess that he wasn't really "a lamb guy." Chicken, he said, was okay, but he didn't eat much red meat. So I regrouped and served a chicken casserole. This recipe had been in my file for years, never used. Turns out I was really overlooking something wonderful. This serves ten easily.

CHICKEN AND ARTICHOKES

  5 Tbsp. butter, divided use

  9 Tbsp. flour

  2 c. chicken stock

  1¼ c. milk

  1 tsp. salt

  Dash each garlic powder and black pepper

  6-8 chicken breasts, cooked, skinned, and sliced—about 5½ c., divided use

  ¼ c. chopped celery

  8 oz. cheddar, grated

  ½ c. mayonnaise

  ⅓ c. fresh lemon juice (don't use that bottled stuff!)

  ½ tsp. lemon pepper

  2 c. artichoke hearts, drained and sliced

Topping:

1 c. soft bread crumbs

1½ tsp. lemon peel, grated

¼ tsp. each garlic powder, salt, and black pepper

Melt 3 Tbsp. butter in large saucepan. Add flour and stir, but don't brown. Add chicken stock and milk and whisk until it boils. Add salt, dash each of garlic powder and pepper. Chop ½ c. of the chicken and add it with the celery. Cook for a minute.

Add cheese, mayonnaise, lemon juice, and lemon pepper to sauce mixture. Cook until cheese melts. Stir sauce thoroughly to blend. Grease a 3-quart casserole—I used a large paella pan—and layer chicken, artichokes, sauce. Repeat layers.

For topping: sauté crumbs in remaining 2 Tbsp. butter. Add lemon rind, garlic powder, salt, and pepper.

Bake casserole 30 minutes in 350° oven.

(Of course, Christian picked out the artichokes, but Jordan and I ate his share.)

Sometimes I like to spend all day Saturday cooking, but other times I want something quick and easy—but good—for company. This is a good marinade for flank steak. (It took me a long time to learn to cut flank steak on the diagonal.)

MARINADE FOR MEAT

¼ c. soy sauce

¼ c. Worcestershire

2 Tbsp. lemon juice

2 Tbsp. chopped fresh cilantro

1 Tbsp. minced fresh ginger

Season a 1½-lb. flank steak. Let the meat sit in the marinade for 24 hours, and it will be better than ever.

COMPANY STEW

My friend Jean Walbridge gave me this, her mother's recipe. It's a good, hearty winter meal and yet one that doesn't require all-day attention.

3 lbs. chuck roast, cut into bite-sized pieces

1 20-oz. can tomatoes

2½ c. tiny peas, or equivalent frozen peas

3 large carrots, scraped and diced (I always use a couple of handfuls of baby carrots)

¾ pkg. boiler onions

½ 10-oz. can beef consommé

½ cup white wine

4 Tbsp. minute tapioca

1 Tbsp. brown sugar

½ cup breadcrumbs

Salt and pepper to taste

Mix ingredients in Dutch oven. Cover and bake at 250° for 6 or 7 hours. Serve over rice or noodles, with fresh green salad, crusty bread, and wine. You could probably do this in a crockpot, too, though I haven't tried it.

P.S.—It's wonderful what tapioca does for some dishes. My mom always threw a generous pinch into meatloaf or chicken loaf to help it hold its shape. You can't tell it's there.

This is also quick and easy, though best if chilled ahead of time, and it's sort of a summer dish.

CRAB LOUIS

Dressing:
1 c. mayonnaise
½ c. sour cream
¼ c. bottled chili sauce
2 Tbsp. lemon juice
Green scallions, chopped
Fresh tarragon or chives, snipped
Combine and refrigerate.

CRAB LOUIS PLATTER
Fresh greens
2 lb. fresh lump crabmeat, picked for shell and cartilage
1 c. diced celery
4 hard-boiled eggs, quartered
Chopped parsley
Capers
Line a platter with greens.
Toss together crabmeat, celery, and dressing. Go easy putting dressing on a bit at a time, so you don't drown the salad.
Arrange salad and quartered eggs on the lettuce. Sprinkle with chopped parsley (flat leaf is best) and capers.

ANOTHER GOOD DRESSING FOR CRAB SALAD

¾ c. mayonnaise

2 tsp. Dijon mustard

1½ tsp. whole grain mustard

1 tsp. tarragon vinegar

½ tsp. Tabasco

2 tsp. drained capers

1 scallion, chopped

Cobb salad is a great choice when you want to serve a light supper. The original Brown Derby Cobb Salad was apparently tossed as a salad, not served "arranged" as it is in many restaurants today.

COBB SALAD

½ head each, leaf and romaine lettuce

½ bunch watercress

3 hard-boiled eggs, chopped

2 skinless chicken breast halves, grilled and chopped

2 tomatoes, seeded and chopped

1 ripe avocado, sliced (dip into lemon juice to keep slices from turning brown)

½ c. crumbled Roquefort or bleu cheese

6 strips bacon, cooked and crumbled

2 Tbsp. chopped chives

Dressing:

½ c. water

½ c. red wine vinegar

Juice of ½ lemon

1½ tsp. Worcestershire

Salt and pepper

½ tsp. sugar

½ tsp. Dijon mustard

1 clove garlic, minced

1½ c. vegetable oil

½ c. olive oil

Make dressing by whisking all ingredients but oils together. Gradually whisk in oils. Refrigerate and stir before using.

For the salad, mix lettuces and watercress in large bowl. Arrange remaining ingredients, except bacon and chives, in strips on top of the greens. Sprinkle bacon and chives over all.

This is best done at the table, for showy effect. Pour the dressing over the salad and toss.

GREEN SALAD WITH TUNA

Another salad I've always liked, particularly for entertaining ladies.

Dressing:

2 tbsp. cider vinegar

1 clove garlic, crushed

¼ tsp. dry mustard

Salt and pepper

⅓ c. oil

Mix all ingredients but oil; whisk in oil; set dressing aside.

Salad:

6 c. torn lettuce and other greens

1 3-oz. can tuna, drained and flaked

2 oz. grated cheese, preferably sharp cheddar

½ c. kidney beans

½ cucumber, cut in chunks

1 carrot, sliced thin

2 radishes, sliced thin

2 hard-boiled eggs, quartered

½ c. sliced tomatoes

Mix salad ingredients together. Pour dressing over and toss. Croutons, homemade or purchased, are a nice addition.

When I want to go casual, I serve burgers on the porch, but I've found recipes for some distinctive burgers.

BLUE CHEESE BURGERS

For people who don't like blue cheese, stuff the burgers with grated cheddar and chopped crisp bacon. But blue cheese is better!

Mix:
1 lb. hamburger
¼ tsp. salt
¼ tsp. garlic salt
A generous sprinkle of pepper
1 tsp. soy sauce
Divide meat into four patties; then divide each patty in half. Flatten each portion into a thin, round circle.
Meanwhile, mix:
½ c. sour cream
¼ c. blue cheese
Top four circles with sour cream mixed with blue cheese. Put other circles on top and crimp edges to seal. Grill.

LAMB BURGERS

1½ lbs. ground lamb
2 minced garlic cloves
3 Tbsp. chopped fresh oregano, or 2 tsp. dried
3 oz. crumbled feta cheese
Salt and pepper
Mix ingredients and form into patties. Season with salt and pepper. Preheat grill or heavy skillet and coat with olive oil. Fry or grill until patties are charred on the bottom. Turn and cook until juices run clear. Serve with tomato slices and lettuce on toasted buns. Mint is good with these, either as a leaf on the sandwich or a bit of chopped mint in the meat.

Sometimes for front-porch dinners I've either served individual baskets or one large serving basket of a mixture of meats, vegetables, and other things. Most of these can be chilled. I line the basket(s) with foil. The table is preset, since this is not finger food and flatware is required. Nor is it one of those dishes where everyone eats out of a common bowl. Guests can dish their food from the basket onto the plate. If you arrange the food in a colorful manner, with an eye to what looks good next to what, you don't need garnishes such as parsley.

For meats, try small lamb chops (1 per person), small pieces of salmon filet, or a half chicken breast grilled (and maybe marinated first) and cut into strips. Surround with cooked, chilled asparagus, cherry tomatoes, baby carrots (maybe blanched for softness), hard-boiled eggs cut in half and sprinkled with herbs or even deviled, scallions, snap peas blanched, half ears of corn— whatever your imagination comes up with. Serve with mayo or a rémoulade mayo. I once served this to a six-year-old who thought it was the best meal he'd ever eaten.

I love to eat in restaurants, and my first thought on going to a new city is, "Where's the best restaurant?" For years, the children and I went to Santa Fe for Christmas, and we found our favorite places. They were not the high-end restaurants for which Santa Fe is famous—Mom couldn't foot the bill for five or more at those. One notable night we walked into Pasquale's, where we had often eaten breakfast, only to find those casual tables covered with white cloths. When I looked at the menu, I must have visibly blanched, because Colin whispered, "Mom, we don't have to stay." And so, staring at the floor, I followed the kids as we trooped out.

We always go to the Guadalupe Café, and I always order the rainbow trout. One night Jordan ordered a burrito but asked for it to come out of the kitchen without chilies. The waiter explained that nothing left their kitchen without chilies, but he would ask them to go light. There was just the tiniest sprinkling of green on her burrito. We also like the Blue Corn Café, where they have great salads, and for some reason we got into the habit of eating sushi one night while in Santa Fe. That ended on the night that several in our party got sick.

And now my grandchildren are cooking. (Morgan)

Breakfast in Santa Fe is a treat. We like Pasquale's, but we really prefer the Tecolote. Megan orders the shepherd's stew or whatever it is they bill as their hottest dish (it doesn't faze her), and I used to order a chicken-liver-and-tomato egg dish until we all learned that chicken livers are bad for you. Now I usually have corned beef hash—not much healthier, but I love it.

I once wangled an assignment to do a travel article that I wanted to call "Down and Out in Santa Fe," but the travel editor renamed it. The point was to show that you could eat well in Santa Fe without breaking the bank. A friend and I tried the margaritas at Maria's (they have some incredible number of flavors) and ate veggie tacos at Baja Taco, hot dogs at Chicago Dog, hamburgers at Dave's Not Here, salads at the small cafeteria in Sanbusco Market, and wonderful meatloaf at Harry's Roadhouse, which has since become a favorite with my family.

In Fort Worth, I usually eat dinner out at least once a week, mostly with my friend Betty. I'm always picking new restaurants to explore and then ending up at old favorites. Café Aspen, where Jamie worked his way

Sawyer

through college, is probably my all-time favorite, although the owner (now a good friend) accuses me of not reading the menu and always ordering my favorites. The Tokyo Café is great for sushi, and Pappadeaux is pretty good for salmon reasonably priced. I look forward to Lobsterama at Lucille's, where you can get a whole lobster with a side salad (the house blue cheese vinaigrette is wonderful) and not eat another bite.

Sheila, my onetime co-author, and I once cooked up the idea of trying out the chef's table at several restaurants. All my friends proved reluctant to spend the money, but Sheila gathered a crowd, and we had a wonderful evening at Joe T. Garcia's in the private dining room where Garcia descendant Lanny Lancarte (one of Jordan's first boyfriends) then served exquisite five- and seven-course meals. (He now has his own restaurant—Lanny's Alta Cocina.) Another time we had a great meal at Bonnell's, where chef/ owner Jon Bonnell impressed us by using a wine sword to open the champagne.

Other people go to movies, theater, and symphonies. I go out to dinner with friends. Good food and good company make a perfect evening for me.

My good friend Betty Boles asked me one night in February 1999 if I didn't want to help out at the Star Café occasionally. The Star is the oldest continually operating restaurant in Fort Worth, having first opened in 1906—Don didn't run it then. I "helped" on Saturday nights for slightly more than six years, with the nice knowledge that it wasn't the kind of job where I had to show up every week. If I

Eden

had a chance to visit grandchildren, I gave advance notice and they found someone else. But most Saturday nights I was there. I liked getting paid in wine and steak or whatever else I wanted off the menu. Sometimes I took a jar of sauerkraut and we made sandwiches of Polish sausage and kraut—one can only eat so much steak!

I finally decided I didn't want to commit Saturday nights, and now I only go occasionally for old times' sake. I'm not a good waitress—I can't "hand carry" (balancing several plates on my arm at one time), and my idea of serving drinks is one in each hand. But I've gotten pretty good at the cash register—okay, everybody makes mistakes sometimes, and then you have to tear the tape off and write "ERROR" on it in big letters.

The Star's world is totally different from the academic one in which I live my professional life, and I made some friends among the staff and a few customers. I still like going there a lot.

The Star is rustic, a steak-and-burgers kind of place that serves the best chicken-fried steak I've ever eaten (I never ate it until I tasted theirs). The counter is scarred, the tables have oilcloth covers, and the chairs are wooden. The walls are covered with all kinds of memorabilia: old photographs, movie posters, a huge and fancy sombrero, old gas stations signs, a sign that says, "Eat Here-Get Gas"—you get the picture. You need to wear jeans and boots when you go there.

In a relatively tiny kitchen, the cooks turn out mouth-watering steaks with a lemon butter sauce, chicken-fried steak that doesn't need a knife, hamburgers that some rate as the best in town. Not much sense giving those recipes, although I will say the secret of the chicken-fried steak is that it's not frozen, pre-battered stuff—they dip and flour it just before cooking. There are a few specialties that are good to share.

On Wednesdays, the lunch special is meatloaf, made by a cook long in Don's employ but according to Betty's recipe.

BETTY'S MEATLOAF

1½ lbs. ground chuck

1 medium onion, chopped

½ green pepper, chopped fine (I'd omit it, but I don't taste it when I eat the meatloaf.)

1 egg, slightly beaten

1 tsp. salt

1 tsp. pepper

18 saltine crackers, crushed

3 8-oz. cans tomato sauce, divided use

Mix well, reserving one can tomato sauce, and put into loaf pan. Top with third small can of tomato sauce. Bake at 350° for one hour. Check and possibly cook for another 15 to 30 minutes.

And when there's meatloaf, there's banana pudding for dessert—again, Betty's recipe.

BETTY'S BANANA PUDDING

    3 egg yolks

    1 c. sugar

    2 c. milk, divided use

    3 heaping Tbsp. flour

    Dash of salt

    2 tsp. vanilla

    2 Tbsp. butter

    Vanilla wafers, 1 small box (not necessary to use the entire box)

    3 bananas, sliced

    Whip cream, sweetened with a little sugar (do not use spray can of whipped cream)

Beat egg yolks with fork until lemony yellow. Add sugar gradually

Separately put 1 c. milk in the top of a double boiler. Allow it to get hot and then skim off the film on the surface and discard.

To the sugar and eggs, alternately add flour and 1 cup milk (not the scalded milk).

Add the above mixture to the hot milk and stir until thickened. Add salt, vanilla, and butter.

Layer vanilla wafers in bottom of stemware alternatively with banana slices and pudding until glasses are full. Serve with whipped cream.

STAR CAFÉ GREEN OLIVE VINAIGRETTE

The Star cooks make the ranch dressing from a mix, but they make it fresh and add their own touch. I don't know what they do to it, but it's really good. The house dressing, vinaigrette with lots of grated cheese and green olives, is made from scratch. It was a bit of trouble reducing it from restaurant quantity to family, but here's the best that Betty and I could do.

    2 c. olive oil

    ½ c. cider vinegar

    ¼ c. lemon juice

    ½ tsp. garlic power

½ tsp. salt

Sliced stuffed green olives, drained

Grated cheddar

Whisk together everything but cheese and olives until thoroughly blended. Add olives and grated cheddar cheese, as much or as little as you want. When I make it at home, I simply leave out the olives. Changes the whole thing, but it's a good vinaigrette, and I like the idea of grated cheddar on salads for a change from Roquefort or parmesan.

It's a great treat to me to eat lunch at Café Aspen or to go there for happy hour and heavy hors d'oeuvres. Owner David Rotman has installed a patio in the last few years—covered and cooled by misters and fans, it's comfortable even in the heat of summer. I love to sit there in the evening with a glass of chardonnay and a plate of smoked salmon. They roll it around cream cheese and serve it with capers and chopped red onion and small crackers. (That menu choice is really why David accuses me of always ordering the same thing.)

My lunchtime rut at Café Aspen involves the spinach-stuffed baked potato, and after numerous requests and threats, David kindly agreed to give me the recipe. He gave it to me in his own handwriting, which is illegible at best. I parsed and figured and estimated and finally had to call him. Here it is:

SPINACH-STUFFED BAKED POTATO

1 large baking potato

Sea salt, pepper, vegetable oil

1 Tbsp. sour cream

1 Tbsp. butter

⅓ lb. finely chopped, sautéed spinach

¼ bunch green onions, finely minced

Pinch of nutmeg

Grated pepperjack cheese

Wash potato and rub with sea salt, pepper, and oil. Bake 45 to 60 minutes at 350°.

Slice off top, taking as little meat as possible, and reserve. Dig out potato meat. While the potato meat is still warm, mix with sour cream.
Cream potato mixture and butter; add spinach, green onions, and a
pinch of nutmeg.

Beat the potato mixture with a mixer (David specifies Kitchen Aid, but . . .)
and stuff it back into the potato shells.

Here's the real trick: at the restaurant, they deep-fry the top that has
been sliced off. Probably too much trouble, but you can fry it in a skillet until its crisp.

Microwave for 2-3 minutes. Top with grated pepperjack cheese and
microwave again, 30 to 40 seconds, until cheese is melted. Replace the
now-crisp top and serve.

Chicken salad is a signature recipe at Café Aspen. It's chunky and good.

CAFÉ ASPEN CHICKEN SALAD

1 lb. chicken pieces, steamed in water with herbs (onions, black pepper, etc.). Dice finely after cooking.

2 celery stalks, chopped

A handful of red grapes, cut in half

2 Tbsp. sour cream

3 Tbsp. heavy mayonnaise

3 Tbsp. lite mayonnaise

Pinch of thyme, salt and pepper to taste. Mix together and chill.

I don't eat out alone much—I don't enjoy it. I have a nice wide circle of
friends, mostly but not all women, with whom I have lunch and (less frequently) dinner. But dinner alone is fine if you've had a bit of sociability at
lunch. Sometimes if I have no lunch plans on a workday, I get tacos from a
place down the street, take them back to my office, and eat and read. But I
don't much like to do it too often.

If I don't have lunch plans on a non-workday, I often go to Central
Market and get myself something really good. Usually it's the tuna salad,

Ford

which I like a lot, and something called Jackson Salad—a mixture of artichoke hearts, hearts of palm, bacon, blue cheese, and onions. If you made that at home, you'd have to buy at least a full can each of artichoke hearts and hearts of palm—no small investment. And then you'd be eating it for a week. I can buy enough for one or two meals. I also like the egg salad—sliced eggs, not diced, with the addition of green peas—a nice touch! Sometimes carefully chosen take-out is a great idea.

In spite of friends, family, and eating out a lot, I eat supper alone four or five nights a week. I manage to avoid some of the obvious pitfalls, such as cereal for dinner or overeating. And I do try to be creative, so that fixing and eating supper is fun. Sometimes I carry my supper for one to the front porch and watch the world go by. But you learn that there are some things you just don't cook for one—like sheet cake! Even if you froze it in single-serving portions, it would last forever and you'd get very tired of it.

I asked other friends what they do about eating alone. One claims that it's because she won't cook for herself and eats out that she can't lose weight. Another said, "When I want meatloaf, I cook it and portion it out in the freezer." I was telling still another friend that someone asked me what you did when you wanted a rhubarb pie. (Since I've never made a rhubarb pie in my life, it's a moot point; my mom made them, but I don't particularly like rhubarb.) Anyway, my friend said when she was divorced and single, she baked a rhubarb pie, ate the whole thing herself, and thought how wonderful it was not to have to share it!

Someone suggested that the freezer is a single person's best friend, but I countered with: "Or your worst enemy." If you freeze a lot of leftovers, you end up with stuff that you don't want to eat but feel you should. Remember that your mom always told you, "Waste not, want not." But freezing often doesn't improve the quality of food—just the opposite. I admit that if I get a yen for sloppy joe or tuna Florentine, I fix it and freeze it—but too often I throw away too much of the leftovers.

I have a partial solution for that: buy a vacuum food saver. Remember the Save-a-Meal machines of the '70s? They sealed food into a plastic bag so that you could freeze it. Trouble is, they left all that air in with the food, and eventually ice crystals formed on it—a sure sign the food is no good. The food saver draws the air out and essentially cryovacs the food. It's great for saving meat—for instance, if you buy a pack of four chicken breasts and only cook one. Vacuum-save the other three individually (the plastic comes in rolls, so you create the size bag you need). Save leftovers, or use the food saver to preserve that really good piece of cheese you bought for a din-

Maddie

ner party but didn't completely use. (Don't freeze the cheese—just keeping air from it will keep that white mold from forming on it.) If you're really smart about using this machine and have the accessories, you can save red wine in the bottle or put things in special jars. (I'm not that smart).

One word, though, about the freezer and food-saving: the airtight seal doesn't last forever, so don't leave leftovers too long, and keep an eye on them. I have two serving-size portions of lamb in the freezer as I write; the seal has broken down, and ice crystals are on the meat. I'll probably pitch them, though right now I just keep eyeing them and choosing something else. (My mother used to think I was far too willing to pitch leftovers.)

Kegan

Baked goods don't work well in the machine—bread, for instance, gets squished because the machine draws air out of the bread as well as the bag. Bread freezes nicely in regular baggies, so you can keep a loaf for a long while. (My kids dispute this and want to refrigerate it, but I insist that it gets stale in the fridge.) When Megan bought a food saver, Brandon tried to "save" everything in the refrigerator. She reported that it was an absolute failure with scallions, which subsequently had to be thrown out. Use some common sense here!

But even with a food saver, leftovers can be discouraging. If you bake lasagna, eat your portion—or maybe three portions in a week—that's still a freezer full of lasagna. So save the lasagna for when the kids come home—or go to the best Italian restaurant you know.

When you cook for yourself, you have to get rid of some long-held notions. One is that "Waste not, want not" dictum that sings like a refrain in our heads. When you cook for one, you're going to waste some food—just pitch it with a clear conscience. It's not waste on the scale that you'd waste food if you cooked for a family of six and had unusable leftovers. Reconcile yourself to both discarding some food and eating the same thing two nights in a row. (If it's good, that shouldn't be a problem.)

A lot of recipes can be reduced to serve two, but it's sometimes hard to reduce them to a single serving. So eat salmon burgers or some other delicacy two nights in a row if you don't want to freeze the other burger.

The other caveat is that you have to learn to shop at a grocery that has a good butcher. I bet you don't buy meat or fish from the butcher because it's more expensive. But you're only cooking for one! It's not that much more expensive. It's better to ask the butcher for one chicken breast than to buy four in a package and have those leftovers. Or use chicken cutlets or tenders instead of a package of breasts. I've been told that the chicken in those pre-packs of four has already been frozen and defrosted; if you take it home and freeze it, you're freezing chicken that is already on its way to getting old.

Want salmon? Buy a one-serving piece.

So many of the casseroles we all enjoyed when we had families are based on cream of mushroom soup. I e-mailed the Campbell Soup company asking if they ever thought of producing half cans of their most popular soups—after all, canned vegetables come in half cans that I find really convenient for myself and for grandchildren. In spite of the protestations on their Web site that all mail is answered within three days, I was still waiting for a reply some months later. I make small bits of white sauce and season it to fit the dish as a substitute for cream of mushroom soup. I haven't tried King Ranch chicken this way yet, but I bet it would work. The Web has recipes for cream soup substitutes, but they are complicated and full of processed ingredients and sound wooden tasting.

Some random ideas:

- Toss cooked tiny pasta with Parmesan, pepper, and a little heavy cream. Add a little chopped parsley for color (even the dried kind).
- Ask the butcher for one or two small lamb chops (if you like lamb) or one pork chop.

- Make an individual pizza, using a flour tortilla as the crust. Top with whatever you want. One I like: spread pesto over the tortilla and top with roasted veggies and goat cheese. Or try a topping of creamed spinach, artichoke hearts, chopped Roma tomatoes, and Parmesan. Invent your own! Bake at 400°, but watch closely so the tortilla doesn't burn.
- Buy those frozen hash browns that can be resealed. Then if you have leftover turkey, for instance, you can make turkey hash. Use bottled or dehydrated turkey gravy to bind together and spice it up with a little garlic powder, Worcestershire, onion, etc.
- Buy sliced turkey in the deli and put it on toast. Cover with cheese sauce or Alfredo sauce and broil. Top with cooked bacon and a tomato slice.
- Some things in the produce department—spinach, broccoli, beans, mushrooms—come loose, so you can buy whatever amount you want. Asparagus doesn't, and that troubled me for a while. It's so expensive, but it's so good. Now I buy a pack of very fresh asparagus (did you know it should be standing in water and not lying on a shelf?) and then I eat it all week—with lemon butter, on buttered toast, chunked up in salad, or even plain.

There are lots of creative things you can do to make your mealtime interesting. For starters, there's tuna. I buy a lot of the 3-oz. cans (one serving—no leftovers), and I do lots of things with this fish that most consider ho-hum at best. The latest word, for healthy eating, is that you should buy chunk light tuna in water rather than albacore, which has more than twice as much mercury because albacore meat comes from older, larger fish that have had longer to absorb mercury. (But the albacore tastes better.)

CREAMED TUNA OR CHICKEN FOR ONE

Make a white sauce of about 1 Tbsp. butter, 1 Tbsp. flour, and a scant ¾ cup milk. Add white wine—more than a splash but less than 1/4 c. because you don't want to make the sauce runny—and a bit of lemon juice. Salt and pepper to taste. Then flake in a drained 3-oz. can tuna. Put in an individual ramekin and cover top with crushed potato chips (stale are fine). Cover the chips with grated sharp cheddar cheese. Bake until sauce is hot and cheese is melted—about 20 minutes at 350°.

When you don't have kids at home, you may not keep milk. I sometimes make a "white" sauce using chicken broth (or bouillon cube broth) and adding white wine for flavor. One night I made creamed chicken this way and stirred in a bit of cream cheese to make it more of a "white" sauce. Lately I've been making the sauce with chicken bouillon and wine, adding tuna, peas, and a chopped scallion, and topping with grated cheese, crushed potato chips, and more cheese. It's delicious—but don't add salt. The bouillon is salty.

TUNA AND PASTA

Cook one serving of orzo, those tiny pastas (I usually just throw a generous handful into the boiling water). Drain and coat lightly with olive oil; flake one 3-oz. can tuna into the pasta. Add capers and their juice to taste. Grate really good parmesan over all. Serve warm. If you like anchovies, add one or two chopped filets. Add chopped parsley for color if you want.

JUDY'S TUNA SALAD

Drain white albacore tuna; season generously with juice of one lemon. Add a chopped scallion and enough mayonnaise to bind. (I am prone to add too much, and it's soupy—then I just dump in some of my favorite food, cottage cheese.)
You can turn this into a tuna melt by putting it on toast, topping it with cheese, and broiling.

TUNA AND APPLES

Use basic mixture but add diced celery; halve the mayonnaise and use a little sour cream. Dice half of a Red Delicious apple and add to the salad.

TUNA WITH MUSTARD

Start with the tuna and lemon and onion, but add one part Dijon mustard to two parts mayonnaise.

In summer, any of these taste great stuffed in a tomato. In winter, I generally just eat them out of a bowl rather than in a sandwich.

BETTY'S TUNA SANDWICHES

One day I was driving to Houston with Betty and Don Boles. Betty announced that she had brought tuna sandwiches, and they were terrific. She mixes tuna, chopped hardboiled egg, finely chopped onion, and chopped sweet pickle. (Betty emphasizes that it is sweet pickle but *not* sweet pickle relish.) Betty didn't give me proportions, but the thing that made the sandwiches so great is that she had a light hand with the onion, egg, and pickle, so that they accented the tuna rather than overwhelming it. I find I have to be careful about that light hand—sometimes I fall into that "more is better" trap, and it's not always true. Moderation in all things.

Serve Betty's tuna on whole wheat bread. I was distressed recently to eat lunch at an upscale country club and find that my tuna sandwich came on processed white bread!

SOUTHWESTERN TUNA

I use this as a dip, served either with crackers or tortilla chips (the good strong kind), but I long ago lost the recipe, so I kind of recreate it each time.

7½-oz. can albacore tuna
Juice of 1 lime (a good juicy one)
2 Tbsp. chopped cilantro
1 Tbsp. capers
¼ c. chopped celery
¼ c. chopped red onion
Pinch of cumin
Mayonnaise to bind

1 can chopped chilies (Use your own judgment about canned chilies or a chopped jalapeño—I like the canned.)

TUNA AND GREENS

Flake tuna with olive oil and serve it over mixed field greens; add fresh green beans, chopped hard-boiled egg, anchovies, and croutons according to taste.

One night my friend Kathie Lang invited Carol Roark and me for dinner and served a great salad that I fix often today. You can fix it for one, or three, or six—whatever you want. This particular night, though, Kathie included shrimp in the salad—and Carol and I are both allergic to shrimp. Kathie still moans about that dinner.

KATHIE'S RICE AND BLACK BEAN SALAD

Rice
Black beans
Assorted vegetables
Vinaigrette dressing
Layer soup plates with rice and then black beans. Top with shrimp or chicken and lots of vegetables, or make it vegetarian, which is what I usually do. Dice cucumber, tomato, scallions, and avocado; slice radishes; sprinkle with green peas and cut green beans. Your imagination is your only limit. Pass vinaigrette when serving so that guests can dress the salad to their own taste. But you can make this for one, and it's great.

SALMON SALAD

Take the small can of salmon (3.5 oz.) and treat it just like the basic tuna, but add chopped cucumber. Or put it on rye bread and layer it with sliced cucumber. You may think you've gone to an English tea.

While I'm on the subject of salmon, fresh salmon is a great treat to me. I never ever thought I'd grind it up before cooking—that is, until I found this recipe for salmon burgers. It serves two, so you'd have one left over. I shared this recipe with my friend Gayla, who keeps a freezer full of what she insists on calling salmon cakes. I warn her that she'll tire of them.

SALMON BURGERS

   10 oz. fresh salmon, ground in food processor
   3 Tbsp. prepared tartar sauce (or make your own of mayonnaise and sweet pickle relish)
   2 tsp. dill
   Salt and pepper
   2 hamburger buns
   Lettuce
   Onion slices
   Tomato slices
   Combine salmon, tartar sauce, dill, salt and pepper, and shape mixture into patties. Grill or sauté until cooked through.
   Sauce:
   ½ c. tartar sauce
   Pinch of dill,
   Grated lemon peel.
   Grill the buns. Serve salmon burger in buns and top with onion slices, tomato slices, and lettuce.

Here are some recipes I've reduced to feed one or two (depending on your appetite):

GROUND BEEF WITH RED WINE

   ¾ lb. ground beef
   Salt and fresh ground black pepper
   1 Tbsp. butter
   2 tsp. chopped shallots
   ⅛ c. red wine
   ⅛ c. beef broth (optional)

2 Tbsp. goat cheese (optional)

Chopped parsley

Shape beef into patties (your appetite determines size). Sprinkle with salt and then press pepper into patties with your hand so that it will stick. Heat a heavy iron skillet without any oil or butter. Sear patties and cook until desired doneness—3-3½ minutes per side leaves them medium rare (the way I like them—but my kids require them more done). Remove from skillet.

Melt butter. Add shallots and cook briefly. Add wine and beef broth and boil until reduced by half. (If you have beef broth granules or an open can, use it; if you'll have to make two cups from a cube to use ⅛ c., forget it.) Stir in goat cheese, if you're using it, and cook until it melts into the sauce. Pour over patties and sprinkle with parsley for color.

One night I had some leftover sun-dried tomato cheese spread and substituted it for goat cheese.

You can do the same thing with half a chicken breast, and it's delicious. In spite of the chicken/white wine and beef /red wine convention, I use red wine when sautéing chicken this way, but I do use chicken broth instead of beef.

A note about red wine: I don't drink red wine, but I keep it on hand for company. If part of a bottle is left, you can refrigerate and use it to cook the next day, but generally it's a waste. For cooking, I buy those little four-packs of individual servings of wine—I call it "travel wine."

Stir-fry is a great thing to do for one, and you don't need a stir-fry pan. A heavy skillet will do fine. I sometimes use nothing more than soy for sauce, but if you want to get fancier, you can make a sauce.

STIR-FRY

1 Tbsp. oil

Small clove garlic, minced or crushed

Vegetables and meat to taste

Soy sauce

Heat oil and add garlic. Then stir fry whatever suits your taste: broccoli, onion rings, green beans, squash or zucchini slices, mushrooms, bell pepper. Sauté in order of firmness—broccoli and onions need to cook before squash, mushrooms, etc. If you want to add spinach or tomatoes, they probably go in at the last minute.

It's your choice if this is a vegetarian dish or not. You can add beef strips (an already tender cut), strips of chicken breast, or even boneless pork. If you use meat, cook it first, remove from skillet, and then return after you cook vegetables.

Sauce:

¼ c. chicken broth

1½ Tbsp. soy sauce

2 tsp. cornstarch

Cook until cornstarch thickens the mixture.

Serve over rice or chow mein noodles. (Chow mein noodles are also a great occasional replacement for croutons in salad.)

BAKED POTATOES WITH LEMON CHICKEN

1 baking potato

½ chicken breast

1 Tbsp. cornstarch

1 scallion, chopped

1 tsp. sesame seeds

Scrub and bake a potato. In the meantime, marinate the chicken in:

¼ c. chicken broth

Generous tsp. of lemon juice

1 tsp. olive oil

1 tsp. white wine

½ tsp. sugar (or less if you want)

Salt, pepper, and garlic powder to taste

Cut chicken into one-inch pieces and toss in the marinade for a minimum of two hours in the refrigerator—longer is better. About 10 minutes before the potato is done, spoon the chicken out of the marinade with a slotted spoon. Sauté in separate skillet until cooked, but not long enough to make it tough. Stir 1 heaping Tbsp. cornstarch into marinade. Add a chopped scallion and boil marinade until it thickens slightly. Stir in sesame seeds and return chicken to the dish.

Split the baked potato and spoon the chicken sauce over it. Lots fewer calories than butter and sour cream.

Here's another veal recipe. Veal is affordable for one but pricey for a crowd—and difficult to serve.

VEAL SCALOPINI WITH GORGONZOLA SAUCE

½ lb. scaloppini.

½ c. beef broth

½ c. chicken broth

Flour, salt and pepper

Olive oil and butter

½ c. heavy cream

¼ c. chopped, seeded Roma tomatoes

½ tsp. dried basil

Tiny bit of tomato paste

¼ c. Gorgonzola

In good-sized skillet, boil ½ c. beef broth (made from cubes) and ½ c. chicken broth until reduced by half. Dredge meat in flour and sprinkle with salt and pepper. Sauté quickly over high heat with olive oil (add a bit of butter and it won't spatter). It takes about 2 minutes per side to cook scaloppini—don't overcook! Add to the meat reduced broth, cream, tomatoes, and basil (if you have fresh, use more), a smidge of tomato paste (buy it in tubes that you can keep in the fridge, so you don't waste a whole can to get a smidge), and Gorgonzola (okay, blue cheese will do).

Sometimes I think my German heritage comes out, for I love those things Mom wouldn't eat. Weiner schnitzel is one of them.

WEINER SCHNITZEL
4 anchovy fillets
1 Tbsp. capers
2 veal cutlets
1 egg, beaten
Fresh breadcrumbs
2 Tbsp. butter
Combine anchovy fillets and capers.
Salt and pepper veal cutlets. Dip first in beaten egg and then in fresh breadcrumbs. Sauté over medium-high heat in butter until golden brown and cooked through—2 minutes per side. Sprinkle anchovy-caper mix over veal cutlets and squeeze lemon juice over them.

I found this recipe for four and cut it down one evening for myself.

LAMB PICCATA
1 blade shoulder lamb chop
    Salt, pepper and flour
    3 Tbsp. butter, divided use
    1 tsp. lemon juice
    Capers
Trim the bones out of the chop, even if it cuts the meat into pieces. Pound thin. Sprinkle with salt and pepper and cover with flour.
Melt 2 Tbsp. butter in skillet and sauté lamb quickly until browned—do not get it overdone. Remove lamb to heated plate (or cover with foil

to keep warm), melt remaining butter in skillet, and scrape up brown bits. Add lemon juice. Pour over chop and sprinkle capers over it.

I have since discovered that you can use the piccata formula on almost anything—flour whatever meat or fish you're using and brown it in a mix of olive oil and butter. (The butter tastes good but burns; the olive oil splatters; a mix controls both.) Remove from pan, add lemon juice and more butter, and pour over the meat. I particularly like this with filet of Dover sole—don't overcook. The sole is thin and cooks through rapidly.

Another quick sauce when you're cooking for one, be it steak, ground sirloin, or a lamb chop: After you've cooked the meat, deglaze the pan with a generous red wine. Add a splash of soy sauce and some goat cheese. Stir until cheese is melted and pour over the meat. So good!

This chicken recipe sort of builds on the popularity of wings but makes them a little less hot than what you get in some restaurants and bars.

CHICKEN BREASTS WITH DIPPING SAUCE
2 boneless half chicken breasts or 1 whole
Milk
Flour, salt and pepper
Butter
¼ tsp. hot pepper sauce
Sauce:
¼ c. mayonnaise
⅛ c. sour cream
1 tsp. water
½ tsp. lemon juice
¼ c. crumbled blue cheese
Pound chicken breast until thin and even. Dip in milk and then flour seasoned with salt and pepper. Sauté until golden—6 minutes a side.

Then toss in 1 tsp. melted butter and ¼ tsp. hot pepper sauce.
Serve with dipping sauce.

This makes two single-person meals.

Nowadays I make the curried chicken salad for one. It's great.

CURRIED CHICKEN SALAD

1 cooked chicken breast half, diced

¼ c. chopped celery

Juice of ½ lemon

¼-½ tsp. curry powder, according to taste

Enough mayonnaise to bind together (you can use part sour cream, if
you prefer)

1 c. grated sharp cheddar

1 c. crushed potato chips

Marinate chicken and celery for an hour in vinaigrette. (I often used
cheap, commercial-brand vinaigrette to marinate, but my favorite brand
for salads is Paul Newman's Own. Jordan once said that our house could
run if we had only cottage cheese, Paul Newman's Own, and white wine—
she put the dressing in the cottage cheese, but that's another story)

Drain chicken. Make a salad by adding curry powder, mayonnaise,
lemon, and sour cream (about twice as much mayo as sour cream).
Chill thoroughly in a refrigerator-to-oven dish.

Mix crushed potato chips and grated sharp cheddar cheese. Top
chicken salad with it and run under broiler until cheese melts. Watch
carefully—the potato chips burn easily.

Here's a great marinade for that single chicken breast you keep buying:

MARINATED CHICKEN

1 chicken breast

1 small clove garlic

2 heaping tsp. chopped onion

1½ tsp. olive oil

⅛ c. soy sauce (or more to taste)

2 tsp. white wine

1 tsp. lemon juice

1 tsp. sugar (or less to taste)

Salt and pepper

½ tsp. dried ginger

Mince garlic clove; add chopped onion, olive oil, soy sauce, white wine, lemon juice, sugar, salt, pepper, and ginger. Use it on shish kebabs, grilled chicken, or whatever. Really nice on grilled chicken fingers served over salad.

CHILLED TOMATO SOUP

1 large tomato

Juice of one lemon or lime

Salt

Chopped chives

1 ear fresh corn, cooked

Wash tomato and put into boiling water for one minute—no longer, no less. Remove and skin. Then seed it. Put remaining tomato in blender and blend until smooth. Add lemon or lime juice and salt to taste. Refrigerate.

To serve, add chopped chives and fresh corn. I used to microwave an ear of corn (three minutes wrapped in cellophane wrap), but I kept hearing about the carcinogenic dangers of combining plastic wrap and the microwave, and I discovered that corn is much better the old fashioned way: boiled ten minutes in water to which you add a pinch of sugar. In this recipe, use half the corn cut from the ear in the soup, and save the other half for another meal.

A Final Word

When I told a good friend at TCU that I was going to be given an award for lifetime achievement, he said, "Does that mean this is the end of it?" I told him I certainly hoped not, and the night the award was presented I quoted that, followed by the words of a colleague who wrote to say, "I definitely know that you are too young for a lifetime achievement award." I liked that a lot better.

But in the same vein, I don't see this memoir/cookbook as the end of a lifetime of cooking. I keep finding new recipes that intrigue me, but you have to stop a cookbook somewhere. So this is where I draw the line. The cookbook is done. I'm not finished cooking.

I still subscribe to *Bon Appetit* and *Southern Living* (absolutely the best for down-home good food), and I still clip recipes from both, though you'd think I have enough in my appalling collection to last a lifetime. I'll still read anything that Ruth Reichl publishes, along with several other writers. These days I get many of my recipes from www.epicurious.com, but I still see cookbooks that I covet—and I put them on my wish list for my children at Christmas. I'll experiment with Texas quail—one of my favorites—but I'll still cook a box cake with the grandchildren. And here is the last recipe in this cookbook.

Maddie, Edie, and I made this cake for my birthday one year. Edie helped a little—there were turf wars over who was pushing whom off the stool, etc.—and I helped a lot more. But Maddie claims credit for the cake. And when it was done, she said in tones of amazement, "Juju, that's the tallest cake I ever saw!"

MADDIE'S TALL CAKE

Make a devil's food cake from a mix; bake in 9-inch round pans. Cool, and put one layer, top side down, on the cake dish. Cover with a filling of:

16 oz. Cool Whip

8 oz. cream cheese

12 Oreo cookies, crushed

That makes a lot of filling and is what makes the cake tall. Put the second layer on top of the filling, bottom side down. Glaze the top only with:

4 oz. melted semi-sweet chocolate

¼ c. melted butter

Easy, pretty, and delicious. Hats off to Maddie!

I said above that I felt the most important thing I've done in this world is to raise four wonderful children. But I think it's almost as important to teach my grandchildren the wonders of cooking, the joy of experimenting with food, and the comfort of fixing old favorites. Today, only a few are old enough to cook with me, but several others are coming along. Of course, I have other things to do—books to write, a press to run—but cooking and passing along its joy are a big part of my life.

Index of Recipes

APPETIZERS

BREADS

BREAKFAST DISHES

CASSEROLES

MISCELLANEOUS

SALADS

SEAFOOD